2 PETER

GROW IN GRACE

The Proclaim Commentary Series

THE PROCLAIM COMMENTARY SERIES

2 PETER
GROW IN GRACE

NEW TESTAMENT
VOLUME 22

MATTHEW STEVEN BLACK

WENATCHEE, WASHINGTON

2 Peter: Grow in Grace
(The Proclaim Commentary Series)
Copyright © 2022 by Matthew Steven Black
ISBN: 978-1-954858-31-2 (Print)
        978-1-954858-32-9 (E-book)

Proclaim Publishers
PO Box 2082, Wenatchee, WA 98807
proclaimpublishers.com

Cover art: *Saint Peter Church in Saint Charles, Missouri*

Unless otherwise quoted, Scripture quotations are from the ESV® Bible (The Holy Bible, English Standard Version®), copyright © 2001, 2016 by Crossway, a publishing ministry of Good News Publishers. Used by permission. All rights reserved.

Scripture quotations marked NASB are taken from the New American Standard Bible®, Copyright © 1960, 1962, 1963, 1968, 1971, 1972, 1973, 1975, 1977, 1995 by The Lockman Foundation. Used by permission.

Scripture quotations marked NKJV are taken from the New King James Version®. Copyright © 1982 by Thomas Nelson. Used by permission. All rights reserved.

Scripture quotations marked NIV are taken from The Holy Bible New International Version®, NIV® Copyright © 1973, 1978, 1984, 2011 by Biblica, Inc.® Used by permission. All rights reserved worldwide.

Scripture quotations marked CSB are taken from the Christian Standard Bible®, Used by permission. All rights reserved. CSB ©2017 Holman Bible Publishers.

Scripture quotations marked NLT are taken from the Holy Bible, New Living Translation, Copyright ©1996, 2004, 2007 by Tyndale House Foundation. Used by permission of Tyndale House Publishers, Inc., Carol Stream, Illinois 60188. All rights reserved.

Scripture quotations marked KJV are taken from the King James Version of the Bible.

All rights reserved. No part of this publication may be reproduced, stored in a retrieval system or transmitted in any form by any means, electronic, mechanical, photocopy, recording or otherwise, without the prior permission of the publisher, except as provided by USA copyright law.

Notes: (1) Ancient quotations have been at times changed to the ESV as well as some archaic language updated, and additional phrases added for clarification. At times verse references (non-existent until recent times) have been interspersed as well to guide the modern reader. (2) We have done our best to be careful in footnoting. Due to the nature of the sermonic material, various items are quoted freely, and may not have proper footnoting. If any great error is noticed, please contact the publisher, and it will be remedied in whatever way is available to us.

First Printing, June 2022
Manufactured in the United States of America

Dedicated to my dear friends and forever family, Pedro and Emily Cerrillos and their daughters: Eliana, Priscilla, Victoria, Casandra, and Linnea.

CONTENTS

INTRODUCTION 13
    Date 13
    Recipients 14
    Message 14
    Outline 14

1 | 2 PETER 1:1-4 OUR RIGHT STANDING 15
    Our Standing in Justification (1:1-2) 16
        Peter's Standing 16
        The Church's Standing 17
        An Equal Standing 18
        The Focus of Our Standing 19
        The Security of our Standing 19
        The Benefits of our Standing 20
    Our Power in Regeneration (1:3) 21
        The Potency of Regeneration 21
        The Sufficiency of Regeneration 21
        The Intimacy of Regeneration 22
        The Excellency of Regeneration 22
    Our Promise of Sanctification (1:4) 23
        The Promise is Predestined 23
        The Promise is Personal 24
        The Promise is Practiced 25

2 | 2 PETER 1:5-7 ADD TO YOUR FAITH 27
    The Foundation (1:5) 28
        A Foundation of Faith 29
        A Foundation of Virtue 32
        A Foundation of Knowledge 32
    The Hard Work (1:6) 33
        The Hard Work of Self-Control 33
        The Hard Work of Perseverance 34
    The Payoff (1:7) 37
        The Payoff of Godliness 37
        The Payoff of Community 38
        The Payoff of Christlikeness 38

3 | 2 PETER 1:8-15 HOW TO GET UNSTUCK ... 41

The Problem of Being Stuck (1:8-11) ... 42
- A Promise to Stop Ineffectiveness ... 43
- A Warning Against Ineffectiveness ... 44
- A Call to Effectiveness ... 46

The Pathway to Being Unstuck (1:12-14) ... 50
- The Importance of Constant Reminder ... 50
- The Importance of Ending Well ... 50

The Power of Being Unstuck (1:15) ... 51
- The Power of Helping Others ... 51
- The Power of Personal Testimony ... 51
- The Power of Christian Education ... 52

4 | 2 PETER 1:16-21 SEEING WITH SPIRITUAL EYES ... 55

Our Walk with Christ (1:16) ... 57
- Christ is Historical ... 57
- Christ is Redemptive ... 59
- Christ is Divine ... 59

The Worship of Christ (1:17-18) ... 60
- The Revelation of Christ Leads us to Worship ... 61
- The Love of Christ Leads us to Worship ... 62
- The Majesty of Christ Leads us to Worship ... 62

The Witness of Christ (1:19-21) ... 63
- The Word is Infallible ... 63
- The Word is Clear ... 63
- The Word is Divine ... 64
- The Word is Authoritative ... 65
- The Word is Spirit-Inspired ... 66

5 | 2 PETER 2:1-10A UNMASKING FALSE PROPHETS ... 69

Realize Their Presence (2:1) ... 70
- False Teachers are Determined ... 71
- False Teachers are Deceitful ... 73
- False Teachers are Disillusioning ... 74
- False Teachers are Damned ... 74

Recognize Their Pretense (2:2-3) ... 75
- Their Attraction ... 75
- Their Activity ... 77
- Their Abyss ... 78

Remember Their Past (2:4-10) ... 79
- Remember the Angels ... 79

Remember the Ancient World 82
Remember Sodom and Gomorrah 84
Remember Judgment Day is Coming.. 86

6 | 2 PETER 2:10B-22 HOW TO SPOT A COUNTERFEIT 91

False Teachers are Arrogant (2:10b-11)................................. 92
Arrogant in Their Character.. 92
Arrogant in Their Contempt 93

False Teachers are Adulterous (2:12-16)............................... 94
Unfaithful in Their Teaching: They Falsify 95
Unfaithful in Their Promises: They Flatter... 97
Unfaithful in Their Dignity: They are Fools 98
Unfaithful in Their Integrity: They Fabricate 98
Unfaithful in Their Morality: They Fornicate 99
Unfaithful in Their Finances: They Fleece... 100

False Teachers are Abandoned (2:17-22) 102
Abandoned to a Fruitless Destiny... 103
Abandoned to Forever Destruction... 104
Abandoned to Foolish Desire 105
Abandoned Futile Damnation 107

7 | 2 PETER 3:1-7 THE LAST DAYS 111

Study the Word (3:1-2)... 112
God's Word Satisfies 113
God's Word Trasforms 114
God's Word Motivates 115
God's Word Demands 117

Shun the World (3:3-6)... 118
The Danger of Scoffers 119
The Depravity of Scoffers 122
The Doubts of Scoffers 122
The Denial of Scoffers... 123

Anticipate the Lord (3:7).. 124
The Consummation is Sudden 124
The Consummation is Sovereign 125
The Consummation is Shocking.. 125

8 | 2 PETER 3:8-13 THE SECOND COMING 129

The Surety of Christ's Coming (3:8-9) 129
Because the Lord is Transcendent 130
Because the Lord is Tenderhearted.. 131

The Shock of Christ's Coming 132
The Suddenness of the End 132
The Severity of the End 133
The Sanctity of Christ's Coming 134
Our Faithfulness 134
Our Focus 134
Our Future 135

9 | 2 PETER 3:14-18 GROW IN GRACE 139

Progress in Your Walk (3:14) 140
Through Patience 140
Through Diligence 141
Through Holiness 142
Through Peace 142
Progress in Your Wisdom (3:15-17) 143
With Steadfastness 143
With Study 143
With Stability 145
Progress in Your Witness (3:18) 146
The Witness of God's Grace 146
The Witness of God's Glory 147

SELECTED BIBLIOGRAPHY 149

ABBREVIATIONS

Common

cf – Latin "conferatur", compare, or see, or see also
ff – and following (pages or verses)
i.e. – Latin "id est", that is
e.g. – Latin "exempli gratia", for example

Books of the Bible

OLD TESTAMENT

Genesis	Gen	Esther	Est
Exodus	Exo	Job	Job
Leviticus	Lev	Psalms	Psa
Numbers	Num	Proverbs	Pro
Deuteronomy	Deut	Ecclesiastes	Ecc
Joshua	Josh	Song of Solomon	Song
Judges	Jdg	Isaiah	Isa
Ruth	Rth	Jeremiah	Jer
1 Samuel	1 Sam	Lamentations	Lam
2 Samuel	2 Sam	Ezekiel	Eze
1 Kings	1 Kgs	Daniel	Dan
2 Kings	2 Kgs	Hosea	Hos
1 Chronicles	1 Chr	Joel	Joel
2 Chronicles	2 Chr	Amos	Amos
Ezra	Ezr	Obadiah	Oba
Nehemiah	Neh	Jonah	Jonah

Micah	Mic	Haggai	Hag
Nahum	Nah	Zechariah	Zech
Habakkuk	Hab	Malachi	Mal
Zephaniah	Zeph		

New Testament

Matthew	Mt	Titus	Titus
Mark	Mk	Philemon	Phm
Luke	Lk	Hebrews	Heb
John	Jn	James	Jas
Acts	Acts	1 Peter	1 Pet
Romans	Rom	2 Peter	2 Pet
1 Corinthians	1 Cor	1 John	1 Jn
2 Corinthians	2 Cor	2 John	2 Jn
Galatians	Gal	3 John	3 Jn
Ephesians	Eph	Jude	Jud
Philippians	Phil	Revelation	Rev
Colossians	Col		
1 Thessalonians	1 Thess		
2 Thessalonians	2 Thess		
1 Timothy	1 Tim		
2 Timothy	2 Tim		

INTRODUCTION

But grow in the grace and knowledge of our Lord and Savior Jesus Christ. To him be the glory both now and to the day of eternity. Amen.

2 PETER 3:18

Peter writes his brief, final reminder to the churches so that his readers will, by God's grace, live in a way that is pleasing to God. In doing so, Peter must also combat the false teachers who were apparently exerting pressure on the churches to depart from the true knowledge of Christ (*cf* chapter 2). The false teaching is not only a theological challenge but also a moral one, promoting some form of sexual permissiveness as a legitimate Christian lifestyle.

Peter identifies himself as an "apostle of Jesus Christ" (1:1). He specifically mentions that he was an eyewitness of the transfiguration (1:16–18; *cf* Mt 17:1–8).

DATE

Second Peter is at the very end of the apostle's life which he references in 2 Peter 1:14. Peter wrote this letter from prison in Rome (*cf* 2 Pet 1:12–15) not too long before his death by execution, around 64 A.D. where Peter is in the Mamertine prison in Rome. Church history records that he was imprisoned with the apostle Paul, and at least one record recounts that they were martyred on the same day in October of 64 A.D., Paul by beheading, and Peter by being crucified upside down. He was offered crucifixion but did not feel worthy to be put to death in the same manner as his Lord, so he made this unusual request, which was accommodated.

RECIPIENTS

Peter is likely writing to the churches of Asia Minor, since Peter mentions that this is his second letter to the same people he wrote to in his first letter (3:1; *cf* 1 Pet 1:1–2). His first letter is addressed to Christians scattered in "Pontus, Galatia, Cappadocia, Asia, and Bithynia" (1 Pet 1:1). These names all referred to Roman provinces in Asia Minor, north of the Taurus Mountains in modern-day Turkey. These territories had been impacted by Greco-Roman culture and had been under Roman control from the mid-first century B.C.

MESSAGE

Peter's theme in his second letter is a simple one: pursue spiritual maturity through the word of God as a remedy for false teaching and a right response to heretics in light of Christ's promised second coming (1:3, 16). When false teachers begin to whisper their sweet words into the ears of immature Christians, the body of Christ begins to break apart, to lose what makes it distinctive in the first place—faith in the unique person and work of Jesus Christ. Peter repeatedly points to the Word of God as the primary means of growth for the Christian (1:4, 19–21; 3:1–2, 14–16).

Peter encouraged his readers to apply themselves to acquiring the true knowledge of God and living out the life of faith with "all diligence," so that they may "be found by [Jesus] in peace, spotless and blameless" (1:5; 3:14). And if believers did not follow his advice, they would be giving their Christian community over to the heretics, people who look to "exploit . . . with false words" (2:3).

OUTLINE

The outline of 2 Peter is fairly simple. Chapter 1 presents us with fruitful Christians. In chapter 2, we are introduced to false teachers. And in chapter 3, we see forward looking Christians who anticipate the second coming of Christ. We might outline it as such:

- The *Pathway* of Christian Growth (ch 1)
- The *Protection* against False Teachers (ch 2)
- The *Preparation* for Christ Coming (ch 3)

Theologically, you could say chapter 1 covers soteriology, chapter 2 covers ecclesiology, and chapter 3 covers eschatology.

1 | 2 PETER 1:1-4
OUR RIGHT STANDING

Make every effort to supplement your faith.
2 PETER 1:5

We remember the story of how Martin Luther was a Roman Catholic monk in Wittenberg, Germany, and how he sought for years, even as a learned teacher of the Bible, to discover peace with God. He was reading through the Bible, searching for peace and couldn't find it. He felt God was angry with him and far away.

The turning point of his life came when he made that journey to Rome. As he was crawling up the stairs of the church in Rome, with tears running down his face, saying the "Our Father" and praying to God for Him to make himself real to him, kissing each stair, while he was climbing to the top of those stairs, suddenly a text of scripture burst into his mind— "the just shall live by faith." In that great and glorious moment Martin Luther understood that it is not by crawling, it is not by kissing, by going to church, nor by human effort, but it is only through faith in Jesus Christ that a man is made right with God.

From that great realization came the spark that ignited the flame that became the Protestant Reformation that spread around the world. We are here today as heirs of the Protestant Reformational tradition because what Martin Luther believed is exactly what we believe today—

that man is justified through faith in Jesus Christ, wholly apart from the works of the law.

Peter starts by helping us understand the power of our justification and then our regeneration and finally our sanctification. The Spirit of God has made us brand new and give us the divine power we need to live the Christian life. All believers are "predestined to be conformed" to the image of Christ (Rom 8:29), and Peter gives us the very foundation of where a holy life comes from.

OUR STANDING IN JUSTIFICATION (1:1-2)

> **2 Peter 1:1** | Simeon Peter, a servant and apostle of Jesus Christ, To those who have obtained a faith of equal standing with ours by the righteousness of our God and Savior Jesus Christ.

Peter here is called "Simeon" which is his given name. "Peter" is a nickname our Lord gave him, and it means "rock" or "stone." He does have a unique office as an apostle who serves the Lord, but he was granted faith. God opened Peter's eyes of faith, and because he came to Christ alone by grace alone through faith alone, he has a right standing with God.

Peter's Standing

> **2 Peter 1:1a** | Simeon Peter, a servant and apostle of Jesus Christ.

Simeon is the Hebrew version of "Simon." "Simeon" is from the Hebrew term *shama*, meaning "Hear" from Deuteronomy 6:4, "Hear, O Israel: The Lord our God, the Lord is one." Simon Peter was not ever known as one who listened very precisely, but instead is known as the apostle with the foot shaped mouth! How was it then that our Lord would give him the nickname "Peter" or "rock"?

It is likely Peter is using his Hebrew designation Simeon as he confronts false teachers in chapter 2, battling with the "circumcision party" that he himself was at one time tempted to follow (*cf* Gal 2:11-14). Peter's repentance is clearly demonstrated at the Jerusalem council where he is the first to declare that salvation is by grace alone through faith alone in Christ alone (Acts 15:6-11).

We see that even in the use of his two names, Peter is letting us know that change is possible. "Simeon" was his old name, reminiscent of his years as a Galilean fisherman; "Peter," the name given him by

Jesus during their first personal encounter (Jn 1:40–42), speaks of the transforming work of Christ that he experienced.[1]

It's also important that Peter is called a "servant" and an "apostle." He's a slave of Christ, and he's one of the original twelve apostles. It shows he is under authority as a slave of Christ, but also one who has authority vested in him, holding the foundational office of an apostle.

Regardless of his service to Christ and his office as apostle, Peter's standing could never hinge on his own works of human righteousness but on "by the righteousness of our God and Savior Jesus Christ." Everything Peter says from this point on in his letter is founded on this glorious standing in the righteousness of Christ.

The Church's Standing

2 Peter 1:1b | To those who have obtained a faith of equal standing with ours by the righteousness of our God and Savior Jesus Christ.

Who is Peter writing to? Peter does not specify the church(es) to whom he is writing his letter. Chapter 3 relates that these believers had collected some of the letters of Paul. His previous letter was written to the "elect exiles of the Dispersion in Pontus, Galatia, Cappadocia, Asia, and Bithynia" (1 Pet 1:1) scattered throughout what is today modern Turkey. Therefore, the best guess is that Peter is writing to Christians scattered throughout Galatia, Asia Minor, Greece, and even perhaps Rome since this is his final letter before he departs to be with Christ through being crucified upside down (according to church history).

Here, however, Peter only identifies them as those who "those who have obtained a faith of equal standing with ours." The term "ours" refers to the apostles, since Peter has just identified himself as an apostle.[2] Though the apostles have walked with Jesus and were eyewitnesses of his resurrection, and though they have such a high place of influence in the church, our standing is equal. The ground is level at the cross. We all come by grace alone through faith alone in Christ alone. We have equal standing because of the "righteousness of our God and Savior Jesus Christ."

---

[1] D. Edmond Hiebert, *Second Peter and Jude: An Expositional Commentary* (Greenville, SC: Bob Jones University Press, 1989), 30.

[2] Allen Black and Mark C. Black, *1 & 2 Peter*, The College Press NIV Commentary (Joplin, MO: College Press Pub., 1998), 2 Pe 1:1.

An Equal Standing

2 Peter 1:1c | A faith of equal standing.

Peter may have had a special office, but we all have "equal standing" before God because of the blood of Jesus Christ. The ground is level at the cross. We see a very tender and humble attitude from Peter in saying this, since he himself had denied the Lord three times and also had almost split the church at Antioch (Gal 2). He understands that his standing is secured by Jesus Christ alone. Just as Christ has keep Peter from falling away, so we have the equal standing and promise as Peter. Our salvation is based on the righteousness of Christ alone. Our only hope of perseverance is based on the work of Christ and our union with him. We call this standing "justification." Paul describes it in Romans 3.

> *Romans 3:24-25* | All have sinned and fall short of the glory of God, ^{24} and are justified by his grace as a gift, through the redemption that is in Christ Jesus, ^{25} whom God put forward as a propitiation by his blood, to be received by faith. This was to show God's righteousness, because in his divine forbearance he had passed over former sins.

Just as the Passover lamb's blood was applied to the door posts of the homes of the believers in Egypt, so the blood of Jesus is applied to the hearts and lives of believers today, and he passes over us. We are justified "by his grace as a gift" by the "propitiation" or "mercy seat" of Jesus. Jesus' blood satisfied the wrath of God. Our sins are not only expiated (cleansed from us) but they are propitiated (justice is satisfied). This is the only righteousness God accepts from sinners. We are therefore justified or declared legally righteous before God's judgment seat. Our standing means we don't have to dread judgment day. On that day, God will wipe away all tears from our eyes.

> *Revelation 21:4* | He will wipe away every tear from their eyes, and death shall be no more, neither shall there be mourning, nor crying, nor pain anymore, for the former things have passed away.

It will be "just as if we've never sinned" except for one thing—the prints of the nails in his hands and feet. He will be like a "lamb slain." Glory and hallelujah, as Fanny Crosby said, "I shall know him by the prints of the nails in his hands." We have nothing to fear. Because of our justification, there is now "no condemnation" for those who are in Christ (Rom 8:1)!

The Focus of Our Standing

> **2 Peter 1:1d** | A faith of equal standing with ours by the righteousness of our God and Savior Jesus Christ.

This right standing all believers have with God is not based on our own performance, but on the righteousness of Christ alone. Peter calls it our "equal standing." We have a righteousness that is not our own, "the righteousness of our God and Savior Jesus Christ." Paul put it another way.

> *2 Corinthians 5:21, NIV* | God made him who had no sin to be sin for us, so that in him we might become the righteousness of God.

Any hope of growth we have comes directly from our entire focus being on the righteousness of Christ. This is God's love gift to us. Any step away from the righteousness of Christ is a step toward sin, anxiety, anger, despair, and foolishness. It is the righteousness of Christ that justifies us and gives us a "standing" with the holy God of heaven.

We need to be clear on the doctrine of justification. It means we are "declared righteous" because of Jesus' death on the cross and his resurrection. He lived the life we could not live. He kept God's law that we could not keep. He took the punishment that we did not want to take. And he rose to life so that we could live in newness of life. He took my rags of sin and gave me his robe of righteousness.

Now because of what Christ has done, you are perfectly righteous in God's sight through faith. God has granted you eternal life and given you the down payment of your inheritance by giving you his Holy Spirit.

The Security of our Standing

> **2 Peter 1:1d** | By the righteousness of our God and Savior Jesus Christ.

How does Christ secure our standing? He saves and keeps us. He is not only our Savior and forgiver of all our sin. He is also our Lord and God. As Savior, he saves us from our sin, and as God, he guides us and keeps us in the faith, walking in a life of holiness. He's predestined us to conformity to himself (Rom 8:29). *Our God and Savior Jesus Christ* is a reference to Jesus alone, and so is important evidence for an early belief in the deity of Christ (*cf* 1:11; 2:20; 3:18 and Tit 2:13).[3] Every knee will bow and confess that he is the Almighty God. He is Yahweh, Creator of heaven and earth and is able to save everyone who comes to him. We will all stand before his tribunal. We will be judged as "righteous," not because of the good works we have done, but according to his mercy and because of his own righteousness applied to our account through faith. Hallelujah.

The Benefits of our Standing

> **2 Peter 1:2** | May grace and peace be multiplied to you in the knowledge of God and of Jesus our Lord.

The benefits of our standing before God in the righteousness of Christ is the grace and peace we experience. Instead of the anxiety and anger and despair that accompany a life of trying to work our way to God, Peter greets the saints first with God's *grace*, that is, God's unmerited favor. We don't have to live in the burden and crushing weight of trying to make ourselves better. We know we cannot change on our own. We can only make ourselves worse. In order to change, we need God's grace. This is God's free gift of a good standing with him. When we make it personal and realize that God's grace was displayed in Jesus' death for me personally, then we are born again. The Spirit fills our heart. And because of this glorious gift of grace, we experience God's *peace*. No longer ought the Christian be harassed by the anxiety and anger of this life or crushed by the circumstances. We can life in perfect peace as our minds are fixed on Christ (Isa 26:3). His grace and peace are "multiplied" to us through a personal knowledge and intimate walk with Jesus our Lord and God.

Our standing in the righteousness of Christ is the very foundation of spiritual growth. The moment our eye is moved away from Christ's righteousness, we begin to be self-reliant, fleshly, and sinful. The odor of anxiety and the noise of frustration fill our hearts since self-righteousness is a stench in the nostrils of God like the stink of filthy, dirty rags (Isa 64:6).

---

[3] David H. Wheaton, "2 Peter," in *New Bible Commentary: 21st Century Edition*, ed. D. A. Carson et al., 4th ed. (Leicester, England; Downers Grove, IL: InterVarsity Press, 1994), 1389.

OUR POWER IN REGENERATION (1:3)

Where does the power come from to grow and change into the image of Christ? Peter tells us we have everything we need because of the indwelling presence of Christ through his Spirit.

> **2 Peter 1:3** | His divine power has granted to us all things that pertain to life and godliness, through the knowledge of him who called us to his own glory and excellence.

Peter is so carried away with enthusiasm for his subject that the Greek is not at its most polished, but the sense is plain. Progress in the Christian life is made possible and practical by two factors: the power of God (1:3) and the promises of God (1:4).[4]

The Potency of Regeneration

> **2 Peter 1:3a** | His divine power...

Without regeneration it is impossible to know and perceive God as he is (Jn 3:3). Regeneration is the new birth that has united us to Jesus Christ. The divine power that operates in believers is of the same divine omnipotence as that which resurrected Christ (*cf* Rom 1:4; 1 Cor 6:14; 15:16–17; 2 Cor 13:4; Col 2:12). That power enables saints to do works that please and glorify God (*cf* 1 Cor 3:6–8; Eph 3:7) and accomplish spiritual things they cannot even imagine (see again Eph 3:20).[5]

The divine power of God is experienced in the believer through the indwelling presence of the Holy Spirit. Paul asks, "Do you not know that your body is a temple of the Holy Spirit who is in you?" (1 Cor 6:19).

The Sufficiency of Regeneration

> **2 Peter 1:3b** | His divine power has granted to us all things that pertain to life and godliness.

Though the divine power of regeneration, we are united with Christ and indwelt by the Spirit. Through this indwelling and union, we have been "granted" "all things that pertain to life and godliness." We lack absolutely nothing (Psa 23:1; Eph 1:3). We are "heirs of God and fellow

---

[4] Ibid.
[5] John F. MacArthur Jr., *2 Peter and Jude*, MacArthur New Testament Commentary (Chicago: Moody Publishers, 2005), 26.

heirs with Christ" (Rom 8:17). This divine power Peter refers to has given us everything we need to live a godly life. We have it through regeneration. Paul tells us that God is able and ready to make "all grace abound" to us.

> *2 Corinthians 9:8* | And God is able to make all grace abound to you, so that having all sufficiency in all things at all times, you may abound in every good work.

God provides everything we need to grow in Christ. Through the indwelling person of the Holy Spirit, all believers are fully equipped with the power of God when they first believe (*cf* Eph. 3:16).

The Intimacy of Regeneration

2 Peter 1:3c | Through the knowledge of him.

We experience the divine power of the indwelling Christ by the "knowledge of him." This is a constant theme in 2 Peter 1. We add to our faith virtue and *knowledge* (1:5). If we don't add to our faith, we may become "ineffective or unfruitful in the knowledge of our Lord Jesus Christ" (1:8). Paul said, "that I may know him and the power of his resurrection" (Phil 3:10). It is that daily knowing of Christ, that love relationship which enables us to experience the power of the divine nature that dwells within us.

The word for "knowledge" here (*epignōsis*) refers not to mere intellectual awareness, or to theoretical knowledge, but to "heart knowledge." Peter and his fellow believers do not merely know *about* God and Jesus; rather, they share an intimate relationship with their God—they literally *know* God through Jesus Christ. The point is that when intimate "heart knowledge" of God through Christ increases, our grace and peace increase as we become more like Christ.[6]

The Excellency of Regeneration

2 Peter 1:3d | Who called us to his own glory and excellence.

God called us and drew us to himself (*cf* Jn 6:44), opening our eyes and granting us eternal life. He called us and drew us to his own glory and moral excellence. "Glory" (*doxa*) here refers to Christ's splendor

---

[6] Charles R. Swindoll, *Insights on James and 1 & 2 Peter*, Swindoll's New Testament Commentary (Grand Rapids, MI: Zondervan, 2010), 269.

and majesty as a divine being.[7] When combined with "glory," "excellence" refers to the divine moral excellence of Christ, focusing especially on the beauty of his goodness.[8] As a result, we have the divine power of the indwelling Spirit, reflected in his own glory and excellence. When he called us, he opened our eyes to the beauty and excellence of his glory. His beauty was irresistible.

> *Revelation 22:17* | The Spirit and the Bride say, "Come." And let the one who hears say, "Come." And let the one who is thirsty come; let the one who desires take the water of life without price.

We heard the call from the Spirit, and the glory of his excellence was overwhelming and overpowering. When the Spirit called, we came running.

OUR PROMISE OF SANCTIFICATION (1:4)

Peter starts by assuring us of our standing in justification and moves to our power in regeneration. But how does our salvation all work out? How do we actually become conformed into the image of Jesus Christ? It is by the sanctifying power of the Spirit's application of the Scriptures to our lives.

> **2 Peter 1:4** | By which he has granted to us his precious and very great promises, so that through them [*promises from the Scriptures*] you may become partakers of the divine nature, having escaped from the corruption that is in the world because of sinful desire.

By the glory and excellence of Christ's person who dwells in us through his Spirit all the promises of his word belong to us. Why? Because he has "granted to us" that it be so.

The Promise is Predestined

> **2 Peter 1:4a** | By which he has granted to us his precious and very great promises.

---

[7] Thomas R. Schreiner, *1, 2 Peter, Jude*, vol. 37, The New American Commentary (Nashville: Broadman & Holman Publishers, 2003), 292–293.

[8] James M. Starr, *Sharers in Divine Nature: 2 Peter 1:4 in Its Hellenistic Context (Coniectanea Biblica New Testament Series, 33)* (Stockholm: Almqvist & Wiksell International, 2000), 43–44.

By knowing the indwelling, abiding presence of the glorious and excellent Christ, we are granted all the promises of God in the Bible. These words include all the divine promises for God's own children contained in the Old and New Testaments (*cf* 2 Cor 7:1), such as: spiritual life (Rom 8:9–13), resurrection life (Jn 11:25; 1 Cor 15:21–23), the Holy Spirit (2:33; Eph 1:13), abundant grace (Jn 10:10; Rom 5:15, 20; Eph 1:7), joy (Psa 132:16; Gal 5:22), strength (Psa 18:32; Isa 40:31), guidance (Jn 16:13), help (Isa 41:10, 13–14), instruction (Psa 32:8; Jn 14:26), wisdom (Pro 2:6–8; Eph 1:17–18; Jas 1:5; 3:17), heaven (Jn 14:1–3; 2 Pet 3:13), eternal rewards (1 Tim 4:8; Jas 1:12).[9] This also includes the land promises to Israel which now belong to us, as we are grafted in to God's people.

We are predestined to be sanctified (Rom 8:29). Every precious and very great promise in the Scriptures point to our sanctification, that we will be conformed into the image of Christ.

The word "granted" has the idea of a permanent bestowal.[10] We are given the "divine nature" of the Spirit within us when he indwells us. It's been granted to us and can never be undone. The Spirit is the very down payment and earnest of our eternal inheritance (Eph 1:13-14). We are now forever given the rights and privileges of being God's very own children (Eph 1:5). What God has done in granting us his promises indicates past action with continuing effects.

The Promise is Personal

> **2 Peter 1:4b** | So that through them [*promises from the Scriptures*] you may become partakers of the divine nature.

Through the *precious and very great promises* in the word of God, we become partakers and participants in the divine nature, which delivers us from a life of sin and sinful desire.

The ancient Christians would call themselves "Christ-bearers" and said partaking of the divine nature is the same as fellowshipping with the Holy Spirit.[11] Today we might say that we are "Jesus with skin on." In other words, the one who later calls us to "add to our faith" is within

---

[9] MacArthur, *2 Peter and Jude*, 30.
[10] Hiebert, *Second Peter and Jude*, 46–47.
[11] Origen, *Fathers of the Church: A New Translation*, "Sermons on Leviticus 4.4.2" (Washington, D.C.: Catholic University of America Press, 1947–), 83:73.

us, empowering and enabling us to grow in Christ (*cf* Phil 2:13). He is not only our Immanuel, God with us, but he is God in us!

The Promise is Practiced

2 Peter 1:4c | Having escaped from the corruption that is in the world because of sinful desire.

For the Christian, we have already "escaped" from the world's corruption because of the sinful desire that once ruled us. While we are not sinless as believers, we are sinning less. Indeed, "sin shall not have dominion" over the true born-again believer (Rom 6:14). We have a new heart whereby the Spirit causes us to walk in his statutes and keep his judgments (Eze 36:26-27; *cf* Gal 5:16). We are called to "keep in step with the Spirit" (Gal 5:25).

It is implied here then that the sinful desire that once ruled us is replaced with a new occupant on the throne of our heart: the Holy Spirit of God. Because the Spirit occupies our heart, giving us new desires, we have escaped the corruption that once had such a strong hold on us through our sinful desires. Praise God that the Spirit has given us a new heart with new desires by which we walk in victory.

Someone has said that sanctification is walking in the justification that Christ has purchased for us. Without having the foundation of a right standing with Christ, everything else crumbles to the ground as a house built on the sand. Therefore, walk in your standing: you are a child of God, and your heart is his abode. "On Christ the solid rock I stand, all other ground is sinking sand!"

Conclusion

Perhaps you have no assurance that you are justified in Christ. Your standing before God frightens you. What should you do? Let me answer that by telling you a story of a young man who was troubled about his soul.

After a series of meetings had finished, the evangelist Billy Sunday was helping the workmen take down the tent. A young man who had been in the meeting the night before came up to Mr. Sunday and asked him earnestly, "What must I do to be saved?"

Sunday said, "You're too late," and kept on working.

"Don't say that" exclaimed the young man, "for I desire salvation; I would do anything or go anywhere to obtain it."

"I can't help it," Sunday replied. "You're too late; for your salvation was completed many years ago by Jesus Christ, and it's a finished work. All you can do is simply accept it. You have done nothing and can do nothing to merit salvation. It is free to all who will receive it."[12]

Just as that evangelist pointed the young man to Christ alone, that's the only hope I can offer as well. Christ said, "It is finished." What was finished? He was finished paying for your sins and mine. We cannot add to the atonement by having perfect faith or perfect repentance. We have to take our eyes off ourselves and place them onto Christ alone. The only thing that can settle your troubled soul is the blood of Jesus. He paid it all! I can add nothing to it. It is totally and completely finished. Anyone who trusts in him for salvation has a right standing with God, adopted into God's family with all the rights and privileges of a true son or daughter.

---

[12] Dan DeHaan, *Intercepted by Christ* (Reno, NV: Cross Roads Boos, 1980), 22.

2 | 2 PETER 1:5-7
ADD TO YOUR FAITH

> *Make every effort to supplement your faith.*
> 2 PETER 1:5

Have you ever been rock climbing? Perhaps you've attempted the indoor wall climbing. I've done neither. I'm afraid of heights. If I ever did try to attempt to climb the face of a cliff, I would definitely want a lifeline retracting security cable as part of my gear. Imagine climbing to the top of a cliff, and you are just about to walk on solid ground, but your foot slips, and you find yourself pummeling to the ground like an episode of Road Runner and Wile E. Coyote. Without a lifeline cable, certain death awaits.

According to the apostle Peter, the lifeline for Christians is the word of God. The key to a fruitful life of progress up the cliff of life, is God's lifeline of truth. We grow into Christlikeness by the grace of God's word and Spirit. This is a passage with severe warnings. If we are not situated firmly with God's lifeline around us, or if we allow friends or circumstances or feelings to cut us away from God's lifeline, we can become blind and fall away from our calling, "forgetting we were cleansed from our former sins" (1:9).

We are called to grow and change into the image of Christ. We have the standing before God so that we are justified. We are righteous in the sight of God because of faith in Christ's work. The ground is level at the cross (*cf* 1:1-4). But that's not the end. It's just the root system of righteousness. We need to see the trunk and the branches, the buds, the leaves, and the fruit. We need to add to this foundation of faith. That's what Peter tells us in this text. For this very reason, since we have a right standing and all the divine power for life and godliness, let's grow! Let's add to our faith!

> **2 Peter 1:5-7** | For this very reason, make every effort to supplement your faith with virtue, and virtue with knowledge, **6** and knowledge with self-control, and self-control with steadfastness, and steadfastness with godliness, **7** and godliness with brotherly affection, and brotherly affection with love.

Perhaps a good illustration to show what is happening here is to think of how an embryo develops in a mother's womb. All the parts of the baby are developing simultaneously. The fingers are forming and growing while the lungs are developing along with the arms and torso, and so forth. Yet even though all the parts are developing at a certain rate all the time, there is a noticeable developmental sequence as well. The brain must be constantly developing, ever regulating the growth of the whole body. So it is with our faith. We have everything we need the moment we are born again. We just need to learn how to use it.

It reminds me of Peter Parker from the Marvel Universe. Remember how Peter Parker became Spiderman? He got bit by a radioactive spider. Understand that the moment he got bit, he had all the power of Spiderman, but not all the skills. He had no idea how to use his powers, but he still had the power. Remember the first time he touched his sink handles? He ripped them off and water spurted everywhere. Remember he got scared and jumped to the ceiling and was stuck there because he didn't know how to release his adhesive hands? He had the power but not the understanding of how to use them.

So it is for every child of God. Peter has just told us that we have everything we need to live the Christian life. "His divine power has granted to us all things that pertain to life and godliness" (2 Pet 1:3). Paul also tells us that we are predestined for holiness in Christ (Eph 1:4; Rom 8:29). So how do we build the foundation?

THE FOUNDATION (1:5)

The first three qualities: faith, virtue, and knowledge, lay a foundation for change. Without a faith commitment to Christ and a desire to please him, we cannot change. These qualities are sequential with each increase by internal growth of the heart, each new grace springing out of, supporting, and perfecting the other. [13] Each subsequent quality balances and brings to perfection the one preceding.[14] These are all aspects of the glory of the indwelling Christ—his character shown in the Christian's character."[15] Peter presents to us an ethical progression that builds toward a climax in Christlike character manifested in love.[16]

A Foundation of Faith

> **2 Peter 1:5a** | For this very reason, make every effort to supplement your faith.

The Object of our Faith

Faith is the beginning of your relationship with Jesus Christ. Faith always has an object, and for Christians that object is Jesus. When we repent and believe, we are born again. This is where transformation begins. "Without faith it is impossible to please God" (Heb 11:16). The object of our faith and trust is the person and work of Jesus. We believe he died for our sins and rose again that we might walk in newness of life. Through this faith we are "born again to a living hope" (1:3; *cf* Eph 2:8-9; Acts 16:31). Saving faith is a free and unmerited gift, granted only to undeserving sinners, according to God's sovereign grace, through which we personally receive an irrevocable share in the full salvation accomplished for us by the Lord Jesus Christ (Eph 2:8). Faith is not a work, but the opposite of a work, it is the receiving of God's free gift of salvation.

> *Romans 4:5* | To the one who does not work but believes in him who justifies the ungodly, his faith is counted as righteousness.

---

[13] J M. R. Vincent, *Word Studies in the New Testament* (McLean, VA: MacDonald Publishing Company, 1886), 324.

[14] J. A. Bengel, *Gnomon Novi Testament*, 1773, quoted in Michael Green, *The Second Epistle General of Peter and the General Epistle of Jude* (Grand Rapids, MI: Wm. B. Eerdmans, 1968), 71.

[15] Stephen W. Paine, "The Second Epistle to Peter," in *The Wycliffe Bible Commentary*, eds. Charles F. Pfeiffer and Everett F. Harrison (Chicago: Moody, 1962), 1458.

[16] J. Daryl Charles, *Virtue Amidst Vice: The Catalog of Virtues in 2 Peter 1* (London: Sheffield Academic Press, 1997), 145–46.

The Substance of our Faith

It's not blind faith. "Faith is the substance of things hoped for, the evidence of things not seen" (Heb 11:1, NKJV). Our conscience, the complexity of creation, and the laws of morality and science demonstrate that faith in the unseen God is rational and reasonable. Indeed, there is no true atheist since God has revealed himself to all men through conscience and creation, so that all people are without excuse.

> *Romans 1:19-20* | What can be known about God is plain to them, because God has shown it to them. [20] For his invisible attributes, namely, his eternal power and divine nature, have been clearly perceived, ever since the creation of the world, in the things that have been made. So they are without excuse.

The Surrender of Faith

Ultimately, saving faith is a commitment to trust and surrender to Christ, no matter how I feel and no matter how impossible and chaotic the situation may be. Our faith is not in our feelings or circumstances, but in Christ alone. We have to begin with our love relationship with Christ before we can have any hope of change.

The Worldview of Faith

Of course, faith includes repentance. Remember the first words of the gospel.

> *Mark 1:15* | The time is fulfilled, and the kingdom of God is at hand; repent and believe in the gospel.

In the New Testament the word translated "repent" means "to change one's mind," and so also "to regret, feel remorse over the view previously held."[17] Repentance therefore is a change of mind and worldview. We see everything differently when Jesus Christ is at the center. We see with new eyes. We hate the sin we used to love, and we love the God we used to hate or ignore. We stop trusting self and we start trusting Christ. This is repentant faith.

---

[17] J. D. G. Dunn, "Repentance," in *New Bible Dictionary*, ed. D. R. W. Wood et al. (Leicester, England; Downers Grove, IL: InterVarsity Press, 1996), 1007.

The Diligence of Faith

True faith is an acting, living faith that brings us to real change in our life. It's important to "make every effort to supplement" the faith God has given us. Diligence is at the heart of faith. Faith has opened our eyes to who God is, so we want to diligently please God and love him with all our heart, soul, mind, and strength (Lk 10:27; cf Deut 6:5).

Making every effort implies haste, eagerness, and determination. It means to apply ourselves as much as possible.[18] God's call to salvation brings with it the power of transformation. He creates the moral excellence he demands. Therefore, it follows that the moral excellence of believers can only be attributed to God's grace. And yet New Testament writers never polarize divine sovereignty and human responsibility. Those whom God has effectively calls to virtue are also to practice virtue with energy and intensity.[19] They are enabled by the Spirit of God who resides within them. Paul gives us an idea of how this works in his letter to the Philippians.

> *Philippians 2:12-13* | Work out your own salvation with fear and trembling, [13] for it is God who works in you, both to will and to work for his good pleasure.

James has told us that "faith without works is dead" (Jas 2:26). Faith works through love (Gal 5:6). Because we have this gift of faith, we work it out in an active and vital way. How? First, by adding virtue. The word to "add" is a fascinating one. It is a vivid metaphor drawn from the Athenian drama festivals, in which a very rich patron, would pay the expenses of choruses and plays.[20] The idea is that we have all the virtue and knowledge and self-control, etc., that we need, because God has already given us "all things" that pertain to godly living (1:3b). Therefore, we should generously add or make a deposit of these godly characteristics into our lives. The first virtue we are to add is virtue itself.

---

[18] Swindoll, *Insights on James and 1 & 2 Peter*, 271.

[19] Schreiner, *1, 2 Peter, Jude*, 299.

[20] Michael Green, *2 Peter and Jude: An Introduction and Commentary*, vol. 18, Tyndale New Testament Commentaries (Downers Grove, IL: InterVarsity Press, 1987), 86.

A Foundation of Virtue

2 Peter 1:5b | For this very reason, make every effort to supplement your faith with virtue.

Virtue is moral excellence, or the desire to please God and imitate him (Eph 5:1).[21] Virtue is our desire to be more like Jesus. To be virtuous is to have a firm and consistent desire to please God in all circumstances, no matter what. It is not perfection but the sincere desire to do all that the Lord asks of you (Ruth 3:11). In order to live out your faith, you first must begin with wanting to please him in all things. That's virtue.

Virtue is something we have immediately upon receiving our new nature in Christ. The Holy Spirit indwells us, and he gives us his desire, changing us to love what he loves.

Ezekiel 36:27, NIV | I will put my Spirit in you and move you to follow my decrees and be careful to keep my laws.

These new desires are holy and virtuous. They are desires for moral excellence, or we might more simply say Christlikeness. The Christian's greatest desire is to be like Christ, pleasing God in all things, more than a baby wants to breathe. The thing that keeps us from growing in Christ is that we get distracted with anger or anxiety, despair of foolish worldliness, and our growth gets stunted. We need to "make every effort to supplement" our "faith with virtue." Yet virtue is not enough for the fully fruitful and mature life in Christ. It's wonderful to have the desire to please God, but we need to know how to please God. We have to research and add knowledge from the word of God to our lives.

A Foundation of Knowledge

2 Peter 1:5c | For this very reason, make every effort to supplement your faith with virtue, and virtue with knowledge.

Knowledge is the receiving the word of God and learning how to apply it. Knowledge completes the foundation, for without knowing God through walking in his word, we wouldn't know how to obey Christ even if we had the desire to obey! We must have knowledge to have mind-renewal (Eph 4:22-26). It is impossible to gain transformational

---

[21] Schreiner, *1, 2 Peter, Jude*, 299.

knowledge from the Bible without knowing its Author. Knowledge comes from knowing the Bible through the revelation of the Holy Spirit of God. We also gain knowledge through fellowship with other Christians, church attendance where the Bible is taught, prayer for more insight, and even reading Christian books and biographies.

These first three qualities must work together to provide a strong foundation for our growth and maturity in Christ, and yet, we might call this high school. How do we get to college? We need to put the knowledge and virtue that we've added to our faith into action. Peter calls that active living out of our faith self-control.

THE HARD WORK (1:6)

Once the foundation is laid, there is a lot of hard work that needs to occur in order to put our faith into action.

The Hard Work of Self-Control

2 Peter 1:6a | And knowledge with self-control.

Self-control is choosing to do God's will which is found God's word, no matter what I feel like. Self-control is gained when we submit ourselves to God to be controlled by the Holy Spirit. We can't do it alone—it requires cooperation!

Adding self-control reminds me of when I first learned to drive a car. I was fourteen, living in Louisiana. I had the desire to drive the car. I had the energy. I had a little knowledge. The first time I drove, I didn't know the difference between the gas and the break, but I learned that really fast. Then I put it into action. It was hard the first time, but the more I practiced, the easier it got. So, it is when we put our faith into practice. We are called to obey God, putting off the old life, and putting on the new life (Eph 4:22-24). We do what pleases God no matter what we feel like, how hard it is, or whatever the circumstances might be. We are not controlled by our emotions or circumstances, but by the Spirit working in us to apply the word of God in any given situation.

One of the assignments I like to give when people are learning how to grow and change, and they don't know how to realistically begin the practice of self-control is what is called the "heart of change journal." The purpose is to find an area of my life that is displeasing to God. You can usually find it because it is taking away a person's peace and enjoyment of God's goodness. A lack of self-control and giving into sin causes misery. Here are some helpful questions I ask and answer in my journal.

- How was I responding in my thinking and acting? (What is the idol indicator...example: anger, anxiety, despair, or foolishness/escape/worldliness)
- What was I wanting or what did I believe would make me happy? What am I worshipping or desiring above God?
- What does the word of God say about my situation, my response, and my source of joy?
- What should I want?
- What did I do to repent?
- Record how you repented and put on Christ.

The principle of self-control is described by Paul in Ephesians 4:22-24 as the "put off, put on" principle. The heart of change journal is meant to change our behavior by first changing our heart and therefore our perspective. For instance, if I am struggling with anger, I need to put on forgiveness, tenderness, and kindness (Eph 4:31-32). If I'm struggling with anxiety, I need to put off other things mastering me and put on trust in God (Mt 6:24-33). If I'm dealing with constant despair, I need to stop thinking God has forgotten me and start believing his promises (Psa 13). If I'm depressed, I need to stop listening to my fallen sinful flesh and start counseling myself with the word of God (Psa 42:5-6). If I'm struggling with worldliness and foolishness, I need to find satisfaction and wisdom in Christ even though my situation may seem out of control (Pro 19:23; Psa 63:3; Pro 1:7). Wisdom comes through fearing the Lord by being intentionally aware of his glorious presence in every situation.

The Hard Work of Perseverance

2 Peter 1:6b | And self-control with steadfastness.

Perseverance is choosing to obey God (self-control) over and over and over again. This steadfastness helps us develop a habit of self-control (1 Cor 15:58). This means we choose to please God over and over and over again. "Though the righteous fall seven times, they rise again" (Pro 24:16). We might define perseverance as clinging to Jesus with all your might and hanging on as long as it takes to be victorious.

Here is an interesting question: who was the greatest failure in history? Let me give you a few hints: he failed 14,000 times to invent Latex. He failed 10,000 times to invent the incandescent lightbulb. Now, I don't know about you, but I'm not aware of anyone else who has failed at anything 24,000 times-and those were just two of his experiments. Over the course of his life, he failed at more than 250,000 attempts at various inventions. Yet he is the most prolific inventor ever known. He patented 1,093 different inventions, including the lightbulb, the stock ticker tape, the phonograph, and the microphone. His name was Thomas Edison.[22] Edison said it well.

> Our greatest weakness lies in giving up. The most certain way to succeed is always to try just one more time. —Thomas Edison

This is what Peter says is the key to spiritual growth. You don't have to be a genius to be committed to perseverance. Self-control and perseverance are the hard work of the sanctification process. They work together to conform us to the image of Christ. The key is: never give up. Perseverance is a gift that all believers possess from the Spirit, since he will complete what he has begun (Phil 1:6), and he predestines us to be "conformed to the image of his dear Son" (Rom 8:29). We are chosen for holiness (Eph 1:4). We have the "never give up" DNA inside us already!

Understand though that endurance is not just passive acceptance of hard and difficult things. It has the idea of courageous endurance that fully defies the obstacles of sin, and thus, is active rather than passive.[23] The Christian who perseveres has courageous and steadfast endurance in the face of suffering or evil, both internal and external.[24]

The apostle Peter looked around him and saw that many believers who had started out right in their Christian experience were being sidetracked by the sensual appeals of the immoral culture around them. In addition, libertine false teachers had begun to convince them that they were free to live any way they wished. The professions of these believers to whom Peter was writing were being eclipsed by their immorality and

---

[22] Bruce Loeffler and Brian Church, *The Experience* (Hoboken, NJ: Wiley Publishing, 2015), 162.

[23] J. Daryl Charles and Erland Waltner, *1–2 Peter, Jude* (Scottdale, PA: Herald Press, 1999), 143.

[24] Richard J. Bauckham, *Jude, 2 Peter* (Waco, TX: Word Books, 1983).186.

worldliness. Outright persecution was not so much a threat as were the pressures of moral degradation. These people had begun well, but Peter wanted to insure that they finished well. He knew that in addition to a resolve to pursue Christlikeness, they would need the knowledge of Christ. In addition, they would need self-control to keep their internal desires from sidetracking them. Furthermore, they would need endurance, the quality that guards the heart.[25]

We are called to persevere in victory over indwelling sinful temptations. Keep getting up and going forward no matter what. We must begin here. We may say "Wretched man that I am! Who will deliver me from this body of death?" (Rom 7:24). It's answered many times in the following verses.

Romans 7:25 | Thanks be to God through Jesus Christ our Lord!

Romans 8:37 | In all these things we are more than conquerors through him who loved us.

Romans 6:14 | Sin will have no dominion over you.

Romans 8:29 | Those whom he foreknew he also predestined to be conformed to the image of his Son.

Romans 8:37 | We are more than conquerors through him who loved us.

Philippians 1:6 | I am sure of this, that he who began a good work in you will bring it to completion at the day of Jesus Christ.

2 Peter 1:10 | If you practice these qualities, you will never fall.

Jude 24-25 | Now to him who is able to keep you from stumbling and to present you blameless before the presence of his glory with great joy, [25] to the only God, our Savior, through Jesus Christ our Lord, be glory, majesty, dominion, and authority, before all time and now and forever. Amen.

We have so much hope! We are not bound to fail but predestined to victory. We are guaranteed holiness if we follow this way of growth. The key is the never-give-up attitude. It's yours in Christ.

---

[25] Charles and Waltner, *1–2 Peter, Jude*, 215.

THE PAYOFF (1:7)

Once the foundation is laid and applying the daily hard work of spiritual disciplines to your life, there is a payoff that results in three qualities: godliness, brotherly kindness, and love.

Abraham Lincoln failed in business in 1831, suffered a nervous breakdown in 1836 and was defeated in his run for president in 1856. Lincoln was no stranger to rejection and failure. Rather than taking these signs as a motivation for surrender, he refused to stop trying his best and trusting the Lord. Of course, in 1861 he became one of the most impactful presidents of our United States. In this great man's words:

> My great concern is not whether you have failed, but whether you are content with your failure. —Abraham Lincoln[26]

How much more important it is to never give up in the Christian life. We may suffer various failures, but God guarantees success if we will persevere. We will develop the reward of Christlike character. Oh, to have the heart of Jesus!

The Payoff of Godliness

There is indeed a payoff of sorts as we consistently apply God's word to our heart and life. As we walk in the word through self-control and perseverance, practicing the presence of God, walking in the Spirit day after day, walking in the word, we will develop a habituated Christlike character.

2 Peter 1:6c | And steadfastness with godliness.

Godliness is the habit of being like God and like Christ, habitually responding in a Christlike way (1 Tim 4:7-16). It is the living out of the truth of God's word from a godly character (Titus 1:1), imitating Jesus Christ.

We understand this kind of habituated behavior when it comes to earthly things, like cars. At one time I didn't know how to drive a car. Now I can not only drive a car, but I can tune the radio, eat a sandwich, and drive the car at the same time. I can drive the car so well that I hardly need to think about it. It's muscle memory and habituated.

---

[26] Abraham Lincoln in Richard Stearns, *Unfinished: Filling the Hole in Our Gospel* (Nashville, TN: Thomas Nelson, 2014), 157.

Godliness is the fruit of laying the strong foundation of faith, virtue, and knowledge and then doing the hard work of self-control and perseverance. A heart of godliness means we no longer need to think about how exactly to apply God's word because we've done it so many times it is now habituated—it comes automatically. We've treasured God's word in our heart (Psa 119:11), so there is a rich store to retrieve as we walk through the trials, troubles, temptations, and tribulations of life.

As we learn and grow in the Lord, and persist in forming new and godly habits, we respond more consistently and automatically in a way that reflects God's character.

The Payoff of Community

2 Peter 1:7a | And godliness with brotherly affection.

Brotherly affection is the idea of being loving and useful to your brother and sister in Christ. Loving the body of Christ is an evidence of the new birth.

1 John 3:14 | We know that we have passed out of death into life, because we love the brothers.

1 John 5:1 | Everyone who loves the Father loves whoever has been born of him.

It's no surprise then that the fellowship of brotherly affection is an evidence of advanced spiritual maturity. As we grow in Christ, we become more and more connected to our forever family in Jesus. The lessons we learn, and the heart changes God brings are not just for us, but we build up the entire body of Christ.

All Christians should be characterized by actively loving and serving one another (Jn 13:35). There should be kindness, tenderness, and forgiveness (Eph 4:31). We are to act toward others as Christ would adding "brotherly affection" to our faith.

The Payoff of Christlikeness

2 Peter 1:7b | And brotherly affection with love.

Love (*agape*) is the evidence of advanced maturity in Christ. To have a heart overflowing with love is to be like Jesus Christ. Love is the mark of full maturity. Love toward God and others is our ultimate goal, and it marks us as true believers (Jn 15:12-13; 1 Jn 3:14-18). This proves

God's love is really in us and that we have truly become like he is, for he is love (1 Jn 4:8). We love God by loving one another. Love is the ultimate expression of Christlikeness. Dear saints, we are predestined to be conformed to the image of Christ (Rom 8:29). If we are truly born again, this pathway of Christian maturity is unavoidable. It is the highest calling we have in life.

If we lay the right foundation (faith, virtue, and knowledge) and then continue in the hard work required to become godly (self-control and perseverance), the payoff (godliness, brotherly affection, and love) will surely come. We are to not become weary in doing what is right (Gal 6:9). He promises us in 2 Peter 1:10 that if we diligently live out these eight qualities we will never stumble! Let us be diligent to make progress on this stairway for sanctification.

Conclusion

A group of tourists visiting a picturesque village walked by an old man sitting beside a fence. In a rather patronizing way, one tourist asked him, "Were any great men born in this village?" The old man replied, "Nope, only babies."

Every person who is a born-again believer starts life as a baby in Christ. Whether the new convert is six or sixty, that person is still a new Christian and needs to grow in the Lord. A baby who never grows is a tragedy. So it is in the Christian life. Those who remain spiritual infants are missing out on the richness of the spiritual food in God's word.

3 | 2 PETER 1:8-15
HOW TO GET UNSTUCK

For if these qualities are yours and are increasing, they keep you from being ineffective or unfruitful in the knowledge of our Lord Jesus Christ.

2 PETER 1:8

Do you feel stuck? There's a behavior that you've tried to stop, but you just can't seem to do it. There's a negative thought-pattern that you have attempted to move on from, but nothing you try ever works. There's a relationship that you want to repair, but despite all your best intentions, nothing seems to make things better. You want to change, but you feel... stuck.[27]

No one wants to be stuck. I personally hate the feeling of being trapped in traffic, stalled in long lines at the airport, blocked in a parking space, or stranded in a Chicago snowstorm. Maybe you are like me and start thinking that the stoplight isn't working because it takes so long before turning green. We have clinical words to describe the anxiety and stress that being stuck produces. "Cleithrophobia" (great spelling bee material) is the phobia of being trapped, locked in, unable to leave, the fear of being stuck. In spite of our strong aversion to being

---

[27] Timothy S. Lane, *Unstuck: A Nine-Step Journey to Change that Lasts* (Epsom, UK: The Good Book Company, 2019), 2.

trapped, countless people—maybe you're one of them— find themselves living unhappily in this most detestable of conditions, stuck in life. [28]

THE PROBLEM OF BEING STUCK (1:8-11)

Peter knows about being stuck. He's been there before. At our Lord's greatest moment of need, Peter, as his chief disciple, denied him three times. Remember he thought he'd never recover? But Jesus pursued him and asked him three times, "Do you love me?" He restored Peter, and if you feel stuck, the Lord will restore you. What's the secret to getting unstuck? Let me share a story that gives us the secret.

Nicholas White, a thirty-four-year-old production manager, was returning from a break on a Friday evening when the elevator in his New York City office building became stuck between floors. He had no watch, no cellphone, no water, and no food—only a pack of Rolaids.

He paced, called for help, banged on the elevator walls, and even tried to climb out through the ceiling. He finally managed to pry open the elevator doors, only to be faced with a brick wall. Nearly two days later, he reached his breaking point. White, not a religious man, prayed for help. At four o'clock Sunday afternoon, almost delirious from thirst and by now resigned to his fate, he heard a voice on the intercom asking if anyone was there. Finally, he was rescued by the paramedics. He had been stuck for forty-one hours. White had no lasting physical side effects from his elevator experience, but by his own admission it left him emotionally troubled. He never discovered why the elevator stopped. In the weeks following his ordeal White lost his job of fifteen years, lost all contact with former coworkers, lost his apartment, and spent all his savings. He later acknowledged, "It wasn't so much the elevator that changed me as my reaction to it." [29]

Listen, we are all going to get stuck from time to time, but how we respond to it is what changes us. Peter tells us how to respond when we are stuck.

---

[28] Mark Jobe. *Unstuck: Out of Your Cave, Into Your Call* (Chicago: Moody Publishers, 2014), 9.

[29] Nicholas White in Rich McHugh and Jonann Brady, *Man Trapped in Elevator for 41 Hours* (New York: ABC News), abcnews.go.com/GMA/story?id=4693690, April 21, 2008.

A Promise to Stop Ineffectiveness

We are all going to have trials and troubles and temptations, but what we do in the midst of those troubles makes all the difference. We have to constantly be in growing mode. If you choose to be distracted by a hurt or a fear, you are going to go a ride that hurts you. You can become "ineffective and unfruitful" even though you know the Lord Jesus Christ.

> **2 Peter 1:8** | For if these qualities are yours and are increasing, they keep you from being ineffective or unfruitful in the knowledge of our Lord Jesus Christ.

Getting unstuck does not mean you need to move to another state, change your marital status, find a new job, switch churches, replace a business partner, alter your hair color, shift your major in college, or drowning out your pain by binge watching your favorite show. It does mean making new choices in the middle of your current circumstances.

Building on your righteous standing in Christ, knowing you are God's child, pursued by his unrelenting love, you have to make a choice. When trouble comes, you have to add to your faith virtue. You have to want to please God in all you do, and go on from there: self-control, perseverance, and godliness. Are you learning how to love God in the midst of trials and temptations? Your knowledge of Christ will become unfruitful and ineffective because you will be choked out by fear and bitterness, depression, and worldliness. Don't allow it! When you see yourself getting choked, you've got to make a choice to get out of that ungodly state of mind.

Nicholas White did not know why his elevator stopped moving, and neither did Troy Fredrickson know at first why he was lying on the floor of his house, barely able to crawl to the door. A few years ago, Fredrickson, chief of a small fire department, and his wife were awakened by their young daughter who was complaining of feeling sick and vomiting. Fredrickson had a slight headache himself. But he helped wash his daughter and prepared a clean bed for her. A short time later, his slight headache became a splitting headache, worse than any migraine he had ever suffered. Fredrickson was climbing the stairs to get some medication when his firefighter training kicked in. He realized what was wrong. He and his daughter were suffering from carbon monoxide poisoning, the result of a malfunctioning furnace. He immediately rushed toward the front door, but Fredrickson passed out before he could reach it. When he came to, he was barely able to crawl to the door and open it. Once outside, he fought to stay conscious until help arrived. "If I had not had the training I have," Fredrickson later reflected, "we could have written it off as the flu and gone back to bed. We would have slept to death."[30]

If you are stuck in the Christian life, it's because you are being choked by something more dangerous than carbon monoxide. You are getting choked by deep rooted patterns of sin and idolatry in your heart. Make a choice to get out of that atmosphere of dread and fear. Stop the anger and holding grudges. Stop fantasizing about running and escaping your circumstances and change your heart. Soften your heart to the Lord. Tell someone about your struggles so they can give you some spiritual oxygen from the word and prayer. Make a choice to please God instead of ignoring your sin. Or you will find yourself "sleeping to death" like the firefighter who almost died of cO2 poisoning.

A Warning Against Ineffectiveness

Peter says that we can become so choked by the pressures of what's right in front of us that we can't see anything else, and we become blind—even forgetting that we are Christians.

> **2 Peter 1:9** | For whoever lacks these qualities is so nearsighted that he is blind, having forgotten that he was cleansed from his former sins.

We all forget things sometimes. It can even be funny, up to a point. But memory loss is often serious, and in the case of one rare form of memory loss - amnesia - sudden. Can you imagine forgetting who you are? I've heard of people who get hit on the head and they have amnesia.

The danger of amnesia. One September day in 2001, a 33-year-old Texas woman named Norene got into her car to go to work. As she tells it, the next thing she knew,

---

[30] Troy Fredrickson in Amy Macavinta, "Fireman's close call underscores danger of carbon monoxide, need for detectors," HJNews.com, January 8, 2012, http://news.hjnews.com/news/article_0f2b6676-39bd-11e1-9f8a-001871e3ce6c.html?mode=jqm.

"There's a freeway here in Dallas and I began driving up the freeway, and I got as far as Denton, Texas, but I didn't know where I was."

The next thing she remembers is waking up in a hotel room in an unknown city, without friends or family. She had no idea why she was where she was.

Norene explains,

"When I woke up the next morning, I sat up and I didn't recognize the room. I didn't recognize the purse that was sitting on the floor, or the clothes that were lying over the chair. I didn't recognize myself in the mirror. I didn't even know my name."

This type of amnesia is very rare and comes on suddenly. It can last for hours or even months and affects only two-tenths of a percent of the population.

What happened with Norene? It took her more than a year to recover her memory. She says,

"You know, I lost 33 years, and I had to slowly regain that back. And it is precious to me. And I've done as much as I can and everything I can to build on that."[31]

Worse than Norene's story is the case of spiritual amnesia. It may be you. At one time you were serving the Lord with gladness, but now you have forgotten that, and all you feel is the pain of anxiety all day, all night, all the time. Or perhaps there was a time when you were growing in Christ, and then something changed—the pressures of your job or marriage or family overtook you. Your health started to slow you down. All the sudden you've got spiritual amnesia. You've forgotten who you are.

You could see so clearly, but now you are blinded. You just can't feel the Lord's presence like you used to because you can't see his hand of grace in your life anymore. You are depressed. It's hard to get out of bed. You are stuck.

Have you ever seen the videos of people who are color-blind, and then they are given special glasses, and they can finally see color? Suddenly, they are weeping because now they know what red is or yellow

---

[31] Susan Spencer, "An Unforgettable Tale of Amnesia," *48 Hours* (New York: CBS News. CBS Interactive, May 3, 2009), cbsnews.com/news/an-unforgettable-tale-of-amnesia.

or green or blue is. Perhaps today your world is in black and white. Peter says, you don't have to remain blinded. There is so much to see, but you have to see through the Lord's eyes. What tears of joy you would have if you could be cured of your spiritual myopia. Let God remove your nearsightedness or even blindness and let him open your eyes to the fullness of joy and freedom. Determine to do whatever it takes to get unstuck.

A Call to Effectiveness

Getting unstuck will take some Holy Spirit empowered effort. It's not the kind of fleshly effort, for nothing good can come from our old nature. It's not about trying harder or doing better. That just leads to more discouragement. Peter calls us to be "all the more diligent." Let's find out what he's talking about.

> **2 Peter 1:10-11** | Therefore, brothers, be all the more diligent to confirm your calling and election, for if you practice these qualities you will never fall. [11] For in this way there will be richly provided for you an entrance into the eternal kingdom of our Lord and Savior Jesus Christ.

You could see so clearly, but now you are blinded. You just can't feel the Lord's presence like you used to because you can't see his hand of grace in your life anymore. You are depressed. It's hard to get out of bed. You are stuck.

The Elect's Activity

> **2 Peter 1:10a** | Therefore, brothers, be all the more diligent to confirm your calling and election.

Our calling to salvation and God's grace of choosing us from the foundation of the world should be tested in our own lives. The true elect of God will confirm that they truly are the elect by following the pathway Peter prescribed. Add to your faith virtue and to virtue knowledge and then add the self-control and perseverance, living out a heart of Christlike godliness. Add to that community of brotherly affection and true spiritual maturity, which is love. Confirming our calling means we follow the pathway Peter prescribed. If we don't, it shows we are not elect, and therefore damned. The appeal to confirm our election is an appeal that goes to the heart of the paradox of election and free will. The New Testament characteristically makes room for both without attempting to resolve the apparent antinomy. So here; election comes from God alone—but man's behavior is the proof or disproof of it. [32]

The Christian life is a life of great diligence, but it is not our own power that grows us. It is Spirit infused power.

> *Philippians 2:12-13* | Work out your own salvation with fear and trembling, [13] for it is God who works in you, both to will and to work for his good pleasure.

Because God works in us, we work out our salvation by his power.

The Elect's Community

2 Peter 1:10b | For if you [*all*] practice these qualities you will never fall.

It's hard to see in our English translation, but Peter is actually saying that this kind of progress in the Christian life is a group effort. You all must practice these qualities together. You cannot add to your faith in isolation. You have to grow in your faith in community. That is, your Christian walk is not just vertical, it is also horizontal. You cannot grow without you edifying others around you, and they are edifying you.

> *Ephesians 4:15-16* | We are to grow up in every way into him who is the head, into Christ, [16] from whom the whole body, joined and held together by every joint with which it is equipped, when each part is working properly, makes the body grow so that it builds itself up in love.

We need each other. We all need connection. I heard the story of a brother in Christ who had visited an orphanage in Mozambique. The director mentioned there was a great shortage of people to hold the babies. The brother asked if he could pick up a baby, about nine months old. He wrote about his story. He writes,

> I glanced at the crib in front of me and there she was, Muyena, staring up at me. I asked the nun if I could pick up the little girl and hold her for a minute. She seemed reluctant. With a heavy accent she hesitantly said, "You may go ahead. But just be ready." When I picked up Muyena she immediately wrapped her little legs around my torso, put her arms around my neck and buried her head in my chest. Occasionally she would peek up at me as she held me tight.

---

[32] Green, *2 Peter and Jude*, 93.

I spoke to her in soft tones, as I had to my own children when they were babies. She obviously did not understand a word of English, but that didn't bother her one bit. I walked around with her for a few minutes until our tour director gently insisted we needed to move on. When I attempted to pull Muyena's arms off my neck I realized how strong that little girl was. She clung to me as hard as her little arms and legs could hold her. When I finally placed her back in her crib, she let out a wail that made all the children stop and look. Her mouth was wide open as she cried with all her little lungs could muster, but her eyes were fixed on me. It was hard to walk out of that room knowing those tears were calling out to me. The director looked at me and said, "Everyone wants to be held by someone." [33]

That orphanage director was absolutely right: "Everyone wants to be held by someone." Orphan babies in Mozambique are not the only ones that long for personal connection. In your city, you can be surrounded by people, competing for parking spaces, crowding into elevators, bumping into strangers on sidewalks, and living with very little space between you and your neighbors yet still feel completely alone.

You can be a stay-at-home-mom with children clinging to your housecoat, a college student with two thousand Twitter followers, a doctor who sees dozens of patients a day, or a bus driver who interacts with hundreds of people every shift and still feel isolated. In fact, the most painful loneliness is the kind we experience when people surround us. Most people living in crowded Chicago suburbs rarely know their next-door neighbors. We sometimes share walls, hallways, elevators, and a common street address but remain strangely isolated from each other. Loneliness is not due to the absence of people but to the lack of authentic connection with people.

That place of connection for the Christian is the church of Jesus Christ. You cannot practice adding virtue and self-control and perseverance to your faith with the help of the body of Christ. Everyone wants to be held by someone. First we need to be held by Christ, but that touch often comes through fellowship with our forever family.

The Elect's Security

2 Peter 1:10b | For if you [*all*] practice these qualities you will never fall.

---

[33] Jobe. *Unstuck,* 48-49.

We are the elect, and as the elect of God with new natures and new hearts, we will live transformed lives. As we live according to our new nature, we will not only confirm our calling, but we will be secured from ever falling away. When Peter says, "if you practice these qualities, you will never fall," he's talking about apostasy, rejecting the faith of Jesus Christ permanently. Now Peter is not saying we won't disappoint or deny the Savior. He did that. But as a righteous person, we fall seven times and get up again (Pro 24:16). The very one who calls us to salvation will do it.

> *1 Thessalonians 5:23-24* | Now may the God of peace himself sanctify you completely, and may your whole spirit and soul and body be kept blameless at the coming of our Lord Jesus Christ. ²⁴ He who calls you is faithful; he will surely do it.

The Elect's Assurance

2 Peter 1:11 | For in this way there will be richly provided for you an entrance into the eternal kingdom of our Lord and Savior Jesus Christ.

Why is it that the elect often struggle with the assurance of salvation, and the most proud hypocrites are offended if you dare suggest they should examine themselves to see if they are truly believers? The elect of God indeed do struggle to have that assurance.

Satan would have every Christian think that there is no way back to a vibrant relationship with God once he or she has fallen and failed him. What Peter has told us though is, "That's not true. Don't believe it. I fell, and I am going to finish well. You can do so too. For God has already given you what you need (1:3, 4). Begin walking the road back (1:5–9). Take care to arrive safely (1:10, 11)." If Peter could preach to us, I think he would say something like, "I know you've fallen. I know you've failed Jesus. So did I. I have also experienced those unwanted companions of guilt and shame. They were once at my heels. But in God there is hope and grace. So, on your feet, ascend the path to heaven."[34]

---

[34] David R. Helm, *1 & 2 Peter and Jude: Sharing Christ's Sufferings*, Preaching the Word (Wheaton, IL: Crossway Books, 2008), 199–200.

THE PATHWAY TO BEING UNSTUCK (1:12-14)

How are you going to bear fruit? Peter makes it clear that we cannot do it alone. We need someone to remind us.

The Importance of Constant Reminder

We so easily forget what we have learned in the Christian life, so we need to be constantly reminded. Peter was willing to be that tool to constantly remind the saints that they need to keep growing every day or they would be backsliding.

> **2 Peter 1:12-13** | Therefore I intend always to remind you of these qualities, though you know them and are established in the truth that you have. ¹³ I think it right, as long as I am in this body, to stir you up by way of reminder.

How are you going to bear fruit? Peter makes it clear that we cannot do it alone. We need someone to remind us. Peter knows he's going to die soon (vs 14). Yet he says, "As long as I am alive, I'll keep reminding you constantly, continually of these vital qualities."

Remember the story of Norene? Well, she did indeed recover her memory! But the way it worked was through constant reminder. She had to look over old photos and videos. She had to get reacquainted with her children. After one year her memory is almost fully restored. For the Christian with spiritual amnesia, you need the constant reminder of the joy of Christ's love. You need the constant reminder that you are most blessed when you are most broken. We forget and we tend toward pride and unbelief. But God says the only way to defeat spiritual amnesia is through constant reminder. And you have to do that every minute, every day, until you die. And then you will end well, like Peter.

The Importance of Ending Well

Peter had failed, but he never fell away from the faith. Peter knew there was coming a day soon where he would never be stuck again! The battle will one day be over. The war will be won.

> **2 Peter 1:14** | Since I know that the putting off of my body will be soon, as our Lord Jesus Christ made clear to me.

Peter did put off his earthly tent and entered into glory in October 67 A.D. He submitted to being crucified upside down. Peter has given the example that a Christian may get stuck and may stumble along the way, but a true believer will not fall away, but will end well. The word is filled with promises of God's preservation of us and the perseverance of the saints.

THE POWER OF BEING UNSTUCK (1:15)

As Peter prepares for his imminent death, he wants to encourage his fellow saints that even a good man or woman can have a serious fall and have a complete recovery. You don't have to stay stuck!

The Power of Helping Others

2 Peter 1:15a | And I will make every effort.

Peter failed, but by the power of God he dedicated every effort of the rest of his days to preaching the love of Christ, and his power of restoration. He didn't want anyone else to fail like he did, so he dedicated everything to helping others get unstuck.

If there's anyone with a testimony of failure, it's Peter. And now he's at his final departure to glory. It's 64 A.D., and he's about to go to his own cross. But he wants us to know that it's possible to get unstuck. Remember he denied the Lord three times. He also almost split the church at Antioch. If there's anyone that's been stuck, it's Peter. Peter recovered. Peter was restored. You can recover. You can be completely restored.

When a person is forgiven much, they love much. God's forgiveness and love spurs us on to love. That kind of effort is kindled by the Holy Spirit and driven by the resurrection power of Jesus so that we can say, it's not mere human effort. God uses us when we are most broken, not when we are the strongest. In fact, Paul says, "When I'm weak, then I'm strong." "When I'm at my weakest point, that's when the power of Christ rests upon me in the most manifest way."

The Power of Personal Testimony

2 Peter 1:15b | So that after my departure you may be able at any time to recall these things.

Peter didn't just give us a book, he lived it out. He went to his death for his faith in Christ. He left us a legacy and a testimony. That's what we are doing when the hard times come, we are leaving a legacy for those who follow after us.

Look at all the good Peter did once he got unstuck! He preached Pentecost and three thousand people were saved. Two books in the New Testament. Numerous churches planted. Peter's legacy is to show us that it's possible to get stuck in horrible ways, but then for God to get us unstuck! Jesus didn't come to call perfect people. He didn't come to call those who think they are righteous, but those who know they are sinners. Peter qualifies. The Bible says that the righteous person "falls seven times" and then gets up again, and again, and again (Pro 24:17). God's people do fall, but we get up.

Peter says, he's going to die soon, but after he departs, he wants them to remember what he's taught them. Who are you teaching? Maybe you are one of those who is waiting to be perfect before you teach anyone. Peter would never have been qualified. We do need to be blameless to teach, but that doesn't mean perfect.

What are you leaving behind for people when you are gone? If you live a life that is unstuck, you will likely have even greater fruit after you are gone than when you lived.

The Power of Christian Education

2 Peter 1:15b | So that after my departure you may be able at any time to recall these things.

Peter was not a scholar or professor. He was one of those "unlearned" uneducated fishermen from Galilee. Galilee was the wrong side of the tracks, the backward part of Israel. That's who God uses to educate for the most part. He doesn't call many strong or many wise. He calls the foolish and the weak. So Peter didn't use his lack of education and sophistication as an excuse.

The saints of Peter's day need to recall the things they learned from Peter. Peter gave them a couple of books in our Bible, not to mention he was the source material for John Mark's Gospel, the Gospel of Mark. The point is we can never truly rely on any apostle or any pastor or elder or teacher. We must rely on God through his word.

Peter's leaving. And one day your elders and pastors will depart in death to glory. Who will you depend on? All Christian leaders, as much as we love them, are not guaranteed to be with you at all times. We cannot say that we will never leave you because God may take us home. But there is one that you can rest in: the living God through the ministry of the Holy Spirit revealed in the word of God.

Your leaders will help you as much as they can. Your fellow Christians will help you as much as they can. But you must become mature. Some of you younger men are called to be pastors and elders because one day we won't be here. Will you stand in the gap? Will you stand in the valley of decision for those around you?

Conclusion

One day my daughter Katie got stuck in the elevator between floors where she had her Bag Pipe Band practice when she was in high school. She was riding and got stuck in between floors. She had seen the movies where people get stuck in an elevator and become frantic, banging on the elevator doors, yelling in the hopes that their voices would get someone on the surrounding floors to come to the aid.

Instead of panicking, my daughter opened a little door in the elevator wall and pulled out a telephone. Immediately she was connected with someone on the outside. She didn't need to beat on the wall to get their attention. She didn't need to speak loudly in the phone to receive their help. She could have whispered, and they would have heard her.

In this world, we're going to get "stuck" in places we aren't comfortable with. We can try to rescue ourselves. We can become frozen with panic and beat against the walls or cry out in dismay. But the way to get unstuck is simple. It starts with faith, a complete trust and surrender of your life to the Lord. Call out to him, and even if you whisper, he will hear every word!

If you are stuck, don't stay paralyzed with fear in the elevator of life. Don't stay stuck in anger or despair. Pick up that heavenly telephone and entrust your life to the Lord. He may send a team of saints from your "forever family" at your local church to help you, but be sure, help is on the way! Whatever you do, don't stay stuck. God wants you to live in freedom and joy. Call out to him and he will be sure to rescue you.

4 | 2 PETER 1:16-21
SEEING WITH SPIRITUAL EYES

No prophecy was ever produced by the will of man, but men spoke from God as they were carried along by the Holy Spirit.

2 PETER 1:21

Twenty years ago, the lights went out in New York City at the worst time. According to the New York Times, at 5:07 p.m. on a bustling Friday, office lights, elevators and computer screens all went dark. The impact rippled through the subway system, as disabled signal lights brought the subway lines to a halt at the height of the evening rush hour. Tens of thousands of stranded.

As it turned out, Commonwealth Edison said, the problem was traced to three electrical lines that just happen to power the entire city. The lines mysteriously shorted out, causing a systemwide dip in voltage.[35]

What would it be like to live without electricity and lights? Imagine living in complete darkness. We sometimes fear in modern times what might happen if the electric grid was attacked or if it failed. But think

---

[35] Christian M. Nichole. "Lights Go out across City for a Few Seconds; Subways Are Halted during Evening Rush." The New York Times. The New York Times Company, December 9, 2000. https://www.nytimes.com/2000/12/09/nyregion/lights-go-across-city-for-few-seconds-subways-are-halted-during-evening-rush.html.

about this. The electric lightbulb wasn't invented until 1882 and wasn't in widespread use until 1900. In 1925, less than a hundred years ago, only half of the homes in the U.S. had access to electricity.

I think we agree that being in darkness is a terrible thing. We are grateful for modern electricity. But how much more grateful are we for spiritual light? Having a connection to God in your spiritual darkness makes all the difference. And we do that through the word of God.

Psalm 119:105 | Your word is a lamp to my feet and a light to my path.

How glorious is it when we can see by God's light, the Bible! How horrific it is not to be able to have spiritual sight. Our spiritual sight is 10,000 times more important than our physical sight. Sin leaves us spiritually blind and unaware that we are blind. The Bible gives us new spiritual eyes to be able to perceive reality from God's perspective.

Spiritual sight is how we perceive God and is infinitely more important to have than physical sight. No one can testify to that more than Fanny Crosby who wrote more than 9,000 hymns, some of which are among the most popular in every Christian denomination. She was physically blind, but spiritually, she could see better than any other person of her generation. She wrote so many that she was forced to use pen names lest the hymnals be filled with her name above all others. What people may not realize is that she was blinded at a very young age. The family doctor was away, and another man—pretending to be a certified doctor—treated her by prescribing hot mustard poultices to be applied to her eyes. Her illness eventually relented, but the treatment left her blind. Her love of poetry began early—her first verse, written at age 8, echoed her lifelong refusal to feel sorry for herself:

> Oh, what a happy soul I am, Although I cannot see; I am resolved that in this world Contented I will be. How many blessings I enjoy, That other people don't; To weep and sigh because I'm blind, I cannot, and I won't.

Fanny Crosby loved the word of God. She zealously memorized the Bible. Memorizing five chapters a week, even as a child she could recite the entire Pentateuch, all four Gospels, the entire book of Proverbs, the Song of Solomon, and many psalms, knowing chapter and verse.

In her lifetime, she put the word of God to songs and hymns that we all love. Among them are Blessed Assurance, All the Way My Savior Leads Me, To God Be the Glory, Pass Me Not O Gentle Savior, Safe in the Arms of Jesus, Rescue the Perishing, and Jesus Keep Me Near the Cross.[36]

Spiritual sight is infinitely more important the physical sight. Oh, I'd rather be physically blind all the days of my life on earth and be able to see Jesus than to be lost and dead and blinded in my sins.

In our passage, Peter tells how he came to see with spiritual eyes by meeting and knowing and worshipping Christ and then writing the inspired word of God.

OUR WALK WITH CHRIST (1:16)

The point of spiritual sight is **to see Jesus Christ and walk with him**. But in order to know him and walk with him, you have to know who he is. Christ is not some myth, but he is historical, he is redemptive, and he is personal. Peter walked and talked with him. He's not a figment of Peter's imagination, like the mythical pagan gods, which are no gods at all. Jesus is the God who entered history, not some myth. Listen to Peter's eyewitness testimony, having walked with him for three and a half years.

> **2 Peter 1:16** | For we did not follow cleverly devised myths when we made known to you the power and coming of our Lord Jesus Christ, but we were eyewitnesses of his majesty.

Peter witnessed Jesus' entrance into history. He witnessed his life, his miracles, his death, and resurrection. He ate with him, spoke with him, heard his preaching, observed his joy and sorrow, and beheld his glory at the Mount of Transfiguration. Our Lord often stayed with Peter at his mother-law's home when he was in Capernaum, so when he says Jesus is not a myth, he's speaking as a firsthand witness.

Christ is Historical

Did Zeus ever enter history? Thor? No, they are mythical gods. With the success of the Marvel franchise, we've realized that these myths can be extremely entertaining, but that's where it ends. No one worships Zeus or Thor or the pantheon of Roman and Greek gods anymore. They are mythical figments of the imagination. Their power today lies in camera tricks and green screens. Fantasy can be fascinating,

---

[36] Warren Dunham Foster. *Heroines of Modern Religion* (New York: Sturgis & Walton Co., 1913), 115ff.

but you would really pity the soul that came out of a movie theater as if it were church. Why? Because these are myths and fantasy. Peter says, following Christ is entirely different than following the pagan gods, because Christ is historical.

> **2 Peter 1:16a** | For we did not follow cleverly devised myths when we made known to you the power and coming of our Lord Jesus Christ.

Christ is no myth but is the God who entered into history. Peter made known his power and his coming. His birth was prophesied. Isaiah said the Mighty God would be born into history.

> *Galatians 4:4-5* | When the fullness of time had come, God sent forth his Son, born of woman, born under the law, ⁵ to redeem those who were under the law, so that we might receive adoption as sons.

The glorious God who exists outside of time and history, entered history, which is truly his story. Flavius Josephus (37—100 A.D.) who lived and died in the first century was a Jewish general turned historian wrote in his *Antiquities of the Jews* that Jesus was a true historical person. Though Josephus never claimed to be a follower of Christ, he writes accurately of him. Consider his words.

> And there arose about this time Jesus, a wise man, if indeed we should call him a man; for he was a doer of marvelous deeds, a teacher of men who receive the truth with pleasure. He led away many Jews, and also Greeks. This man was the Christ. And when Pilate had condemned him to the cross on his impeachment by the chief men among us, those who had loved him at first did not cease; for he appeared to them on the third day alive again, the divine prophets having spoken these and thousands of other wonderful things about him: and even now the tribe of Christians, so named after him, has not yet died out.[37]

Josephus affirms what Peter is saying. Jesus is historical. Not only that, his miracles are not magic or myths, but he actually healed people. His life miraculous birth was prophesied. Peter says, "I'm not making this up. I'm an eyewitness." Jesus was human. He walked among us in history.

---

[37] Flavius Josephus. *Antiquities of the Jews* (A.D. 93), 18:3:3. Also see F.F. Bruce. *The New Testament Documents: Are They Reliable?* (Grand Rapids, MI: Eerdmans Publishing Company, 2003), 111-112.

Christ is Redemptive

2 Peter 1:16b | When we made known to you the power and coming of our Lord Jesus Christ.

Peter says, we made known to you his power and his coming. For Peter, Christ is not just some character on a page, but he is an actual person that existed before the world began and took up residence on this earth. Peter walked with him and saw how he fulfilled the law perfectly. He loved his enemies. As they crucified him, he cried, "Father, forgive them." He lived what he preached, and he lived it perfectly.

Jesus' power and coming were prophesied in the Old Testament. Beginning with the books of Moses, we hear about a Savior coming who will crush the serpent's head (Gen 3:15). In Exodus and Leviticus we learn about a sacrificial system with goats and lambs and bulls offered daily, but when Jesus' coming takes place, he is called the "Lamb of God who takes away the sin of the world" (Jn 1:29). He came and died for the sins of guilty men and women, boys, and girls—unworthy people like you and me. Peter knew the eyewitnesses of his birth. Maybe he even had opportunity to interview their friends. Maybe even the shepherds. Being from Galilee, Peter must have heard the story of Christ's miraculous birth from Mary herself on various occasions. He saw him die, and he saw the power of his resurrection. He also made know the power of Christ at his second coming that was yet to occur. Peter taught that Christ could return at any moment, which he paints in glorious imagery later in his epistle (*cf* 3:8-13).

The point is, Jesus comes in power to saved. Jesus saves! He is not just a historical religious figure. He's God in human flesh who died for mankind. He came on a mission and has the power and authority to redeem anyone who comes to him in humble, repentant faith.

Christ is Divine

2 Peter 1:16c | But we were eyewitnesses of his majesty.

Peter now refers to the transfiguration experience he had with Jesus when he revealed his glory to Peter, James, and John. The Greek word for "majesty" is a very rare New Testament word. In every reference, it means the majesty of the divine (i.e., Lk 9:43).[38] It's a word

---

[38] Green, *2 Peter and Jude*, 104.

referring exclusively to God in the New Testament. It's an obvious reference to the unveiled glory of Christ that he had with the Father before the world existed.

Jesus had predicted that some of the apostles would see the manifestation of his divine greatness.[39]

> Matthew 16:28 | Truly I say to you, there are some of those who are standing here who will not taste death until they see the Son of Man coming in his kingdom.

Soon after Jesus said this, he took Peter, James, and John—his inner circle—to a mountain and revealed his glory to them (*cf* Mt 17, Mk 9, and Lk 9). You see Christ is not just human, he is divine. He revealed his eternal attributes to his disciples. There, before their very eyes, Jesus was transfigured in brilliant and translucent light. On either side of Jesus stood the great Hebrew prophets Moses and Elijah.[40] What's the point Peter is making? This one who entered history is the God of history, the Almighty who has power over life and death, power enough to bring two of the greatest figures of the Old Testament with him. Jesus Christ is the Word from the beginning. As John says:

> John 1:1-3 | In the beginning was the Word, and the Word was with God, and the Word was God. ²He was in the beginning with God. ³All things were made through him, and without him was not any thing made that was made.

Jesus is historical; he's redemptive, and he is God almighty. Peter walked with him when he entered into history to save mankind. Peter goes on to describe not only his walk with Christ, but his worship of Christ.

THE WORSHIP OF CHRIST (1:17-18)

Peter had enough spiritual sight **to worship Jesus Christ.** That's why we are given a new heart and new eyes from the Holy Spirit—God wants us to worship his Son in all his power and glory. Peter goes on to describe the transfiguration event.

---

[39] MacArthur, *2 Peter and Jude*, 60.
[40] Helm, *1 & 2 Peter and Jude*, 215.

The Revelation of Christ Leads us to Worship

2 Peter 1:17a | He received honor and glory from God the Father.

Peter, James, and John witnessed the moment the Father recognized Jesus as the Son of God. What a revelation! They could never have understood the vast glory of Jesus had he not revealed himself to them. He received glory and honor from the Father and was revealed to be the glorious Son of God before their very eyes. They worshipped him because he revealed himself to them. In fact, no one can know and worship Christ unless he reveals himself to them.

> *Matthew 11:27* | No one knows the Father except the Son and anyone to whom the Son chooses to reveal him.

We are all naturally blinded to God. Through sin, we have transferred authority of our lives from God to the devil.

> *2 Corinthians 4:4* | The god of this age has blinded the minds of unbelievers, so that they cannot see the light of the gospel that displays the glory of Christ, who is the image of God... ⁶ For God, who said, "Let light shine out of darkness," has shone in our hearts to give the light of the knowledge of the glory of God in the face of Jesus Christ.

Indeed, the Father himself must initiate our coming in faith to him.

> *John 6:44* | No one can come to me unless the Father who sent me draws him.

I got to go to the Mount of Transfiguration, but I didn't need a miracle to see Christ revealed to me. I didn't hear the voice of the Father from heaven, though that would have been amazing. I heard the voice of the Spirit calling in my heart.

> *Hebrews 3:7-8* | The Holy Spirit says, "Today, if you hear his voice, do not harden your hearts."

What joy then does the Christian have when our eyes can see, and our ears can hear! How glorious to once be blind, but now to see. The ancient pastor and theologian Aurelius Augustine rejoiced when God opened the spiritual eyes of his heart. Listen to his praise.

> You called, you cried, you shattered my deafness, you sparkled, you blazed, you drove away my blindness. You shed your fragrance, and I drew in my breath, and now I pant for you. I tasted, and I now hunger

and thirst. You touched me, and I now burn with joy because of your peace.[41]

When Christ reveals himself to us, we cry out with joy and thanksgiving, like the woman at the well, telling all her family and friends to come see Jesus.

> *John 4:29* | Come, see a man, which told me all things that ever I did: is not this the Christ?

God must grant spiritual sight, or we could never see, but when we do see, we rejoice and worship. How can we not praise his name?

The Love of Christ Leads us to Worship

Imagine the joy of hearing the Father's love declared over his beloved Son. The Father gives the Son as a gift to the world, that whoever trusts in him will have eternal life. The Father is "well pleased" in the Son's perfectly fulfilled mission.

> **2 Peter 1:17** | For when he received honor and glory from God the Father, and the voice was borne to him by the Majestic Glory, "This is my beloved Son, with whom I am well pleased."

When Peter, James, and John saw Jesus' glory, they worshiped him. They set up three tabernacles, if you remember, one for Jesus and also for Moses and Elijah. God the Father, here given the title "the Majestic Glory" wants Jesus alone to be worshipped. Suddenly Moses and Elijah are gone, but the voice comes out of heaven that this is God's beloved Son, and they are to worship only Jesus. We are to love Jesus with the same love that the Father has for his beloved Son.

The Majesty of Christ Leads us to Worship

> **2 Peter 1:18-19a** | We ourselves heard this very voice borne from heaven, for we were with him on the holy mountain. **19** And we have the prophetic word more fully confirmed, to which you will do well to pay attention as to a lamp shining in a dark place.

Can you imagine, seeing Christ in all his majesty? Perhaps you might say, "It sure would be much better to be there where Peter was,

---

[41] Saint Augustine Bishop of Hippo, *The Confessions of St. Augustine*, trans. E. B. Pusey (Oak Harbor, WA: Logos Research Systems, Inc., 1996), Book 10, chapter 27.

then I could really worship Christ. If I could just experience all his majesty, power, and glory. Then I could have a closer walk with him."

Listen you have a more fully confirmed word of prophecy than the very transfiguration. The Bible is where you can experience the majesty of Christ in an even greater and surer way than Peter did that day he saw Christ revealed.

THE WITNESS OF CHRIST (1:19-21)

A final reason God gives us spiritual sight is to witness for Jesus Christ.

> **2 Peter 1:19** | And we have the prophetic word more fully confirmed, to which you will do well to pay attention as to a lamp shining in a dark place, until the day dawns and the morning star rises in your hearts, [20] knowing this first of all, that no prophecy of Scripture comes from someone's own interpretation. [21] For no prophecy was ever produced by the will of man, but men spoke from God as they were carried along by the Holy Spirit.

The point of spiritual sight is to see Jesus Christ and witness for him. We see Jesus in the Bible, which is more sure than the miracles and even the transfiguration itself.

The Word is Infallible

> **2 Peter 1:19a** | And we have the prophetic word more fully confirmed.

Peter says that God's word is more fully confirmed than miracles. The theological term for this is infallibility, that is, it cannot fail. God's word will fulfill all it promises. It is a more sure word of prophecy, Peter says, than even the glorious transfiguration of Jesus. How is that possible?

The Word is Clear

Peter says we need to pay attention to God's clear word to light our path. The light of God's word will show us the way.

> **2 Peter 1:19b** | To which you will do well to pay attention as to a lamp shining in a dark place, until the day dawns and the morning star rises in your hearts.

By his word, the Bible, the Lord has spoken to us in a way that is understandable. That doesn't mean that everything is the clearest that it could be. That's why the main thing is the plain thing, and the plain thing is the main thing. Or to put it another way, if the plain sense makes sense, seek no other sense.

God's word gives us wisdom and direction and light when we cannot see. It's like the dawn in the morning as the sun rises. Let Christ the Morning Star, the Sun of righteousness rise in your hearts through the word.

Psalm 119:105 | Your word is a lamp to my feet and a light to my path.

How precious is the word? Does it mean anything to you? Some hardly read it today, but in the year A.D. 303, the Roman Emperor Diocletian issued a decree which he hoped would extinguish the spreading flames of Christianity. One of his primary objectives was the seizure and destruction of the Bible. Later that year, officials enforced the decree in North Africa. One of the targets was Felix, Bishop of Tibjuca, a village near Carthage. The mayor of the town ordered Felix to hand over his Scriptures.

Though some judges were willing to accept scraps of parchment, Felix refused to surrender the word of God at the insistence of mere men. Roman authorities finally shipped Felix to Italy where he paid for his stubbornness with his life. He laid down his life rather than surrender his Bible.[42]

The Word is Divine

The Bible came from God. It is divinely inspired. Peter says that "men spoke from God."

2 Peter 1:20a | Knowing this first of all, that no prophecy of Scripture comes from someone's own interpretation. [21] For no prophecy was ever produced by the will of man, but men spoke from God.

Men spoke from God. That means the Bible is not a collection of human ideas. It wasn't someone's "own interpretation" of how things should be. It wasn't produced by man's will, but by God's will and by the direct hand of God. That means it's powerful! It was not produced by the ideas of men, but men spoke from God. He used their

---

[42] Bruce L. Kelly, *Christian Theology in Plain Language* (Nashville, TN: Word Books, 1985), 41.

personalities, but he guided and breathed out the message and guarded them from error.

Since the word is divine, it is perfectly designed to change your life. Psychology is not only not sufficient, but also often deceptive and deviant. Medications are often dispensed as a cure all. People are angry and disappointed. Regardless of medical conditions, we need medicine for our soul. God designed you, and he made his word to treat the ailments of your soul.

> *Hebrews 4:12* | For the word of God is living and active, sharper than any two-edged sword, piercing to the division of soul and of spirit, of joints and of marrow, and discerning the thoughts and intentions of the heart.

In the book "How God Used D.L. Moody," his assistant R.A. Torrey said the divine word of God was D.L. Moody's secret to fruitfulness. He was not an educated man. He wasn't a sophisticated man. He was a weak and desperate man who depended on the divine word of God. Torrey said the consumption and application of the Bible is the secret to real Holy Spirit power. His words make a strong point.

> You may talk about power; but, if you neglect the one Book that God has given you as the one instrument through which he imparts and exercises his power, you will not have it. You may read many books and go to many conventions, and you may have your all-night prayer meetings to pray for the power of the Holy Ghost; but unless you keep in constant and close association with the one Book, the Bible, you will not have power.

> And if you ever had power, you will not maintain it except by the daily, earnest, intense study of that Book. Ninety-nine Christians in every hundred are merely playing at Bible study; and therefore ninety-nine Christians in every hundred are mere weaklings, when they might be giants, both in their Christian life and in their service.[43] — R. A. Torrey

You want power? You need the God-breathed word of God.

The Word is Authoritative

Because the Bible came from God, every word is authoritative.

---

[43] R.A. Torrey, *Why God Used D. L. Moody* (Edinburgh, UK: CrossReach Publications, 2015), 15-16.

2 Peter 1:20 | Knowing this first of all, that no prophecy of Scripture comes from someone's own interpretation.

Men spoke from God, and therefore the word carries the authority of Almighty God. It is God-breathed, so you will be judged by the word. Since God spoke it, you and all mankind are obligated to follow it.

2 Timothy 3:16 | All Scripture is breathed out by God and profitable for teaching, for reproof, for correction, and for training in righteousness.

The Word is Spirit-Inspired

Because the Bible came from God, every word is authoritative. Those who wrote Scripture were not giving their own ideas, but they were carried along, like a ship on the ocean waves, by the Holy Spirit of God.

2 Peter 1:21 | For no prophecy was ever produced by the will of man, but men spoke from God as they were carried along by the Holy Spirit.

Are you neglecting God's word in your life? What about your children? You cannot depend on the local church to bring your children to Christ and worship with them. Church is one day a week, but you are to worship with your children every day. Sunday school does not replace family worship. And what about you? Do you have a hunger and thirst that you are fulfilling every day? Are you in God's word consistently, not for mere duty, but because you need the Lord? Job said, I need the Bible more than food.

Job 23:10 | I have treasured up the words of his mouth more than my necessary food.

Matthew 4:4 | Man shall not live by bread alone, but by every word that comes from the mouth of God.

It would be better to starve from physical food than to neglect the word of God.

When I was a kid, we were so poor living in Louisiana that the welfare man, Mr. Haney would give us double the free cheese and free butter. One of the reasons I liked going to school is I could get a hot lunch there with red beans and rice, jambalaya or gumbo. I had friends who were even poorer than me, and they learned what hunger pains were.

Dear saints, do you have an appetite for God's word? Are you hungry to know Christ better? Are you sick of the hunger pains of the world?

When my twin sister was younger, lost in her sins and without Christ, she really struggled with anorexia. She had plenty of food, but she wouldn't eat it.

I think there is some spiritual anorexia going on. You've got the word of God right in front of you, loads of spiritual food, but you are starving.

Maybe you've been so depressed for so long you've forgotten the joy of the Lord. Maybe your bitterness is eating you up, and you've forgotten the goodness of God. I'm asking you to dive back into the word and prayer on a personal level. Lead your family there. Stop living with hunger pains. Dive into the word. Get some encouragement from someone in the body so you get into it "day and night" (Psa 1:2).

Conclusion

Peter says, "I saw the Lord on the Mount of Transfiguration." I experienced him. He's not a myth. He's the Son of God. I walked with him. I saw him die and rise again. I saw him! And that made all the difference, didn't it? What about you? Can you see the Lord? We see the Lord through the word of God, and we are changed into his image. Look to Jesus, and you will be transformed!

> *2 Corinthians 3:18* | We all, with unveiled face, beholding the glory of the Lord, are being transformed into the same image from one degree of glory to another.

"Blinding Laser Weapons" are weapons that are designed to blind soldiers on the field of battle. Most countries adhere to international law to minimize the power of their lasers. China, however, instead of limiting the power of such weapons, took full advantage of the potential, developing the battery-powered Portable Laser Disturber. Its desired effect was to injure or dizzy the eyes of enemy combatants. By seeking to blind the enemy, they render them completely unable and unfit to fight. A soldier doesn't have to be destroyed in order to be rendered useless. Blinding them is enough.[44]

---

[44] Sebastien Roblin, "China's Laser Guns: Everything You Always Wanted to Know about Them." The National Interest. The Center for the National Interest, May

Satan doesn't have to get rid of us to take us out of the battle. All he needs to do us render us useless by blinding us to the truth.

12, 2018. https://nationalinterest.org/blog/the-buzz/chinas-laser-guns-everything-you-always-wanted-know-about-25806.

5 | 2 PETER 2:1-10a
UNMASKING FALSE PROPHETS

But false prophets also arose among the people, just as there will be false teachers among you, who will secretly bring in destructive heresies, even denying the Master who bought them, bringing upon themselves swift destruction.

2 PETER 2:1

We remember the 1930s film "The Wizard of Oz" which is really not about the wizard, but about Dorothy. She learned that "there's no place like home." One of the pinnacles of the movie is when we find out that the wizard isn't a wizard at all. He's just a pretender. He's a traveling circus act that got lost flying in his hot air balloon. His famous quote was, "Pay no attention to the man behind the curtain." He was pretending to be someone with great power.

So it is with false teachers today. They want to take advantage of God's people. They will use every deception to do it. But in reality, they have no power unless you give it to him by believing their lies. As the father of lies (Jn 8:44), Satan is constantly using deception and false doctrine to attack the church—employing false teachers to infiltrate the true flock. Claiming to teach truth, these purveyors of demonic error disguise themselves as angels of light (cf. 2 Cor. 11:14), attempting to creep into the fold unnoticed. As a result, throughout redemptive history, God has repeatedly warned believers to be on the alert against such men (and women).[45]

Second Peter does sound awfully gloomy and doomy. As you read through it, it's just full of very intense and dire warnings and constant discussions of destruction and judgment. Before you get turned off to parts of the Bible like this, just remember that very often the most loving thing to do is to warn, and the most positive thing you can do is be negative. Sometimes the most positive thing you can do is be negative.[46]

REALIZE THEIR PRESENCE (2:1)

False teachers are present in all ages as representatives of Satan, trying to take hold of the sheep and keep the lost from coming to Jesus. They profess to know the Lord, but they deny him in their deeds.

> **2 Peter 2:1** | But false prophets also arose among the people, just as there will be false teachers among you, who will secretly bring in destructive heresies, even denying the Master who bought them, bringing upon themselves swift destruction.

"False prophets" means they falsely claimed to be prophets, or that they prophesied false things; and sometimes both. The men were as untrustworthy as the message they preached.

In Israel there were false prophets among the people as well as true; and now history was repeating itself. Peter's readers had false teachers in their midst.[47]

Those who have strayed from this center of orthodoxy have been regarded as outside the true Christian faith. Some of those core truths include:

- the inspiration and inerrancy of Scripture
- one eternal, triune God in three persons: Father, Son, and Holy Spirit
- the undiminished deity and true humanity of Jesus Christ

---

[45] MacArthur, *2 Peter and Jude*, 67–68.
[46] Timothy J. Keller, "The Dangerous Life" Studies in 2 Peter—August 15, 1993 from 2 Peter 2:1–9, *The Timothy Keller Sermon Archive* (New York City: Redeemer Presbyterian Church, 2013).
[47] Green, *2 Peter and Jude*, 115–117.

- Christ's virgin birth, sinless life, substitutionary death for sin, miraculous bodily resurrection, and literal future return
- the special creation and fall of humanity
- salvation by grace through faith
- the eternal life of believers and condemnation of unbelievers

Are such false teachers saved? According to what Peter writes in this chapter, we can conclude that those guilty of teaching doctrines at extreme odds with classic orthodoxy are not, in fact, Spirit-regenerated believers.[48] Those who deny or twist the person and work of Christ are not believers. But they are determined to bring people into their influence, just as they have been of old.

False Teachers are Determined

2 Peter 2:1a | But false prophets also arose among the people, just as there will be false teachers among you.

False teaching really is as old as time. It started in the Garden of Eden with the deceptive serpent. There have always been false prophets.

False prophets arose among the people of Israel. Those people have had their false prophets from the beginning. As soon as they left Egypt, they were deceived by Balaam to worship the fertility god, Baal Peor of the Moabites (*cf* Num 25). Balaam led them into sexual sin related to their false worship of Baal that haunted them their entire existence until the captivity.

As the father of lies (Jn 8:44), Satan is constantly using deception and false doctrine to attack the church today—employing false teachers to infiltrate the true flock.[49] False prophets are determined at all times, in every age, to bring God's people into sin. Their teachings may seem plausible, but they will lead you away from Christ into lawlessness. They will always give you many excuses not to live a holy life. Don't let them come near, for they are determined and present in every age, ready to trap you. Watch out for them!

Today, false prophets preach many false gospels. Here are a few of them. They will preach the false prosperity gospel as well as the poverty gospel. They are both dangerous. The prosperity gospel says that

---

[48] Swindoll, *Insights on James and 1 & 2 Peter*, 287–288.
[49] MacArthur, *2 Peter and Jude*, 67.

because you are God's child you will not suffer but be prosperous in all things. Your prosperity and health are signs of your faith. The poverty gospel says you should vow to be poor. Both are dangerous because we are stewards of whatever God has given us, great or small.

There is the false gospel of self-help, that the Bible is a manual for psychology, to make you feel better about yourself. It's false because we don't exist to feel good, but to glorify God in all we do.

There is the false gospel of signs and wonders. This teaches that if you were truly saved then you'd speak in tongues and see miracles, and if you had enough faith, you can be healed and you can heal others. Tongues and miracles are not signs of salvation, but they are gifts for some of the saints. If you want to verify the presence of the Spirit in every believer, then you must look for the fruit of the Spirit, which is a heart transformed to the image of Christ. Let's realize that not everyone speaks in tongues, and while God loves to grant miracles, he also brings many of his saints to Christlikeness through suffering.

There is the social justice gospel. While all Christians ought to be against racism and inequality, the social justice gospel's solution is not the cross, but the cancel culture. The only solution for injustice is justification by the blood of Jesus. As believers we seek for people to be saved by the blood, since it is the cross of Jesus Christ that justifies. His Holy Spirit can tear down the walls of hostility. We believe that God can save racists, and that the new birth is the solution to all the inequalities on earth. We also believe that ultimate justice occurs after this life, when we see God face to face.

There is the legalism gospel. If I pray the sinner's prayer and change my outward lifestyle, I must be a Christian. This is merely repackaged Phariseeism. True believers understand that real transformation begins with the new birth in the heart. You can change the outside, and never really change at all.

There is the easy-believism gospel. It says 1-2-3, pray after me, and you are in the kingdom. It is a false gospel because it requires no true heartfelt repentance, only acknowledgement of the facts. Even the devils acknowledge the facts about God, and they tremble. Satan himself believes in that way.

False Teachers are Deceitful

False teachers are active, just as they have always been. They are secretly bringing in lies into the church. Peter calls them "destructive heresies."

> **2 Peter 2:1b** | There will be false teachers among you, who will secretly bring in destructive heresies.

A heresy is a false teaching that divides the saints. The term "heresies" denotes "an opinion, especially a self-willed opinion, which is substituted for submission to the power of truth, and leads to division and the formation of sects."[50]

False teachers specifically promote heresies that are "destructive" and damnable. The fact that the heresies are destructive means that they lead to "utter ruin" and speaks of the final and eternal condemnation of the wicked. If a person believes them, they will end up in eternal destruction in the lake of fire. They are usually heresies that give people assurance of salvation, even though they are living lawless lives.

False teachers are never honest and straightforward about their operations. After all, the church would never embrace them if their schemes were unmasked. Instead, they secretly and deceptively enter the church, posing as pastors, teachers, and evangelists.[51] According to Paul, false teachers will disguise themselves as angels of light and servants of righteousness.

> *2 Corinthians 11:13-15* | Such men are false apostles, deceitful workmen, disguising themselves as apostles of Christ. [14] And no wonder, for even Satan disguises himself as an angel of light. [15] So it is no surprise if his servants, also, disguise themselves as servants of righteousness.

Satan comes, not as some scaly monster with horns and hooves and a pitchfork. But he comes as an "angel of light," standing declaring ideas as an apostle or faithful pastor, but he's really a false teacher. He's a wolf in sheep's clothing.

---

[50] W. E. Vine, *An Expository Dictionary of New Testament Words*, 4 vols. (London: Oliphants, 1940; reprint, Chicago: Moody, 1985), 2:203.

[51] MacArthur, *2 Peter and Jude*, 71.

False Teachers are Disillusioning

2 Peter 2:1c | Even denying the Master who bought them.

These false teachers preach the blood of Christ and grace. They proclaim that Jesus paid it all, and they claim to belong to Jesus, because he bought them. But they misunderstand grace. Grace is not a license to sin. These false teachers deny the Master who bought them by the licentious lives they live. There are false prophets who teach the gospel of freedom but live in slavery. God's grace never gives us a license to sin. Romans 6 tells us that God's grace is the power over sin.

> *Romans 6:14-15, 22* | Sin will have no dominion over you, since you are not under law but under grace. [15] What then? Are we to sin because we are not under law but under grace? By no means! [22] But now that you have been set free from sin and have become slaves of God, the fruit you get leads to sanctification and its end, eternal life.

We as true believers are free not to sin! Perhaps you know of someone who, when confronted about his or her adulterous relationship, simply said, as if it were a matter of fact, "Well, I'm under grace, so you can't condemn me." Or maybe the person has shown no desire to stop a lifestyle of sin and defends himself or herself by saying, "God's grace covers me." This is the sentiment of false teachers. They live contrary to sound doctrine.

It can be disillusioning to hear about men of God who have preached the truth but have lived in the filth of immorality. Don't be surprised. Peter warned that false teachers would come, denying the Master that bought them. Don't be discouraged, true sheep will not live contrary to Christ, but will follow Christ. The righteous may fall, but they get up every time, dragging their sin into the light with repentance, and never denying their Master.

False Teachers are Damned

2 Peter 2:1d | Bringing upon themselves swift destruction.

The goal of the false teacher is to bring in destructive, or damnable heresies. These are teachings that give false assurance to the people in the pews. Remember the words of Jesus about these false teachers.

> *Matthew 7:21-23* | Not everyone who says to me, 'Lord, Lord,' will enter the kingdom of heaven, but the one who does the will of my Father

who is in heaven. ²² On that day many will say to me, 'Lord, Lord, did we not prophesy in your name, and cast out demons in your name, and do many mighty works in your name?' ²³ And then will I declare to them, 'I never knew you; depart from me, you workers of lawlessness.'

A lost person can feign faith and even become a pastor or a Christian leader and lie and call Jesus "Lord, Lord." The false prophet who is not ordained by God can do signs and wonders and never know the Lord. He can be a false prophet by teaching false things, or he can be a false prophet by teaching the right things with a lascivious and immoral life. We've heard of these men who are so eloquent in explaining the faith, but we find out that their lives are lawless. Jesus has a message for them. "You may claim to know me, but I never knew you. Depart from you immoral, lawless person."

RECOGNIZE THEIR PRETENSE (2:2-3)

How do false teachers get so many followers? They "have a form of godliness" but they "deny the power" that brings holiness in their lives.

Their Attraction

False teachers have lives that are lustful and lasciviousness. Many are strangely attracted to a life where you can say you love Jesus and live whatever way you want. Peter says that many people are attracted to false teachers and will follow after their shameful ways.[52]

> **2 Peter 2:2** | And many will follow their sensuality, and because of them the way of truth will be blasphemed.

These false teachers sound so good, but inside the reek of serving self and sinful desire. They may give stirring sermons, but their personal lives are devoted to feeding their immoral lusts.

They preach the false gospel of "do what thou wilt" and never speak of "thou shalt not," so they attract many. Multitudes follow their sensual ways, believing the false gospel of cheap grace. They turn the grace of God into lasciviousness (Jude 1:4). This causes people to blaspheme the true Christians who are living holy lives.

---

[52] David Walls and Max Anders, *I & II Peter, I, II & III John, Jude*, vol. 11, Holman New Testament Commentary (Nashville, TN: Broadman & Holman Publishers, 1999), 125.

Attracted to License

I've seen this play out in two extremes. First, you have those who believe grace is a license to sin. The term for "sensuality" is a vivid Greek word for blatant immorality with no shame.[53] Further, it has the idea of:

> An attitude of not recognizing divine authority, and moral codes in society, seeing no need for restraint, and instead, penchant for excess.[54]

We see this in the churches that love every new fad. They are trying to copy the world. They emphasize a kind of cheap grace where the saints are just as sinful as the unbelievers. They celebrate God's forgiveness without any real repentance or change. God's job is to forgive, so their false gospel is one of antinomianism, lawlessness. You just keep on sinning, and God keeps on forgiving.

Attracted to Legalism

Another extreme is one of legalism. They emphasize outward change with little attention to inward change. As long as you are following all the rules, you are considered to be right with God, even if you are living a double life. What ends up happening is they keep all the rules and look great on the outside, but often these teachers are incredibly immoral with little or no accountability. They live in sensuality with legalism as a covering.

Deceived by Liars

I might mention one other deceptive type of false teacher, and we'll call this one the liar. This is the kind of false teacher that uses sound doctrine to cover their lascivious living. This is probably the most devastating kind of false teacher because they actually teach in ways that edify the saints, but they live contrary to what they teach. When they are discovered, the saints are most devastated and confused, and the lost have more reason to blaspheme the name of Christ. Peter says, "the way of truth will be blasphemed" or slandered. It literally means, "to injure the reputation of someone." The reputation of Christ and the

---

[53] William Barclay, *The Letters of James and Peter*, 2nd ed., The Daily Study Bible Series (Philadelphia: Westminster, 1960), 377.

[54] Andrew M. Mbuvi, *Jude and 2 Peter, A New Covenant Commentary*, (Eugene, OR: Cascade Books, 2015), 73.

Christian way of truth is brought to discredit when those who say they identify with Christ involve themselves in obvious immoral behavior.[55]

Sadly, the scandals in the lives of false teachers seem to attract more and more people to the false gospel of license.

Instead, be Devoted to the Living God

Neither license nor legalism nor liars please God, but love for God from the heart.

> *Luke 10:27* | You shall love the Lord your God with all your heart and with all your soul and with all your strength and with all your mind, and your neighbor as yourself.

Let the love of God consume you and holiness will follow! Oh, that we may love God and live holy lives for him with complete surrender and devotion to our holy God.

Their Activity

False teachers love themselves, and because of that, they love to exploit the sheep. They are not in the ministry to help the kingdom of God expand. They want to expand their own kingdom.

> **2 Peter 2:3a** | And in their greed they will exploit you with false words.

They love power and money. Underlying their love for money, false teachers may have a fascination with false doctrine, rebelliousness, or even a penchant for sexual immorality. To be sure, they actively participate in each of those activities. But people can do all such sins without being teachers. Instead, the primary motivation driving false teachers is an unbridled love of money. Later in this chapter Peter describes false teachers as "having a heart trained in greed" (2:14). They crave as much money as possible (*cf* 1 Tim 6:3–5, 10) and are experts at bilking people in the church out of their wealth. This is a standard biblical indictment and characterization of religious charlatans (*cf* Jer 6:13; 8:10; 1 Tim 6:3, 5, 9–11; Titus 1:7, 11; 1 Pet 5:1–3; Jude 11, 16).[56]

They use "plastic words." False teachers love the earthly comfort that power and money can bring, because in the end its all they have. False preachers and teachers use "false" or literally "plastic" words. In

---

[55] Walls and Anders, *I & II Peter, I, II & III John, Jude*, 125.
[56] MacArthur, *2 Peter and Jude*, 78.

keeping with its etymological roots, *plastic* originally had the connotation of something not completely authentic. After all, plastic items often masquerade as another substance, such as wood, metal, china, and so forth. Thus, plastic at first glance "deceives" consumers. In a similar way, false teachers deal in heretical doctrine that masquerades as truth. Their theology is often plausible but twists the word of God (*cf* Col 2:8, 20–23; 2 Tim 2:14–18).[57]

They promote themselves. They "exploit" the sheep for their own kingdom and their own gain, but that's all they have. Their skill is exploiting the sheep, forming their "plastic" fake doctrine to suit the ears of the hearers, giving what they want.

Their Abyss

Their end is coming swiftly. Damnation, Peter says, is hunting them down. False teachers may think they are living the high life, but God will take them down.

> **2 Peter 2:3b** | Their condemnation from long ago is not idle, and their destruction is not asleep.

Peter reiterates that the *condemnation*, pronounced against false teachers long ago in the Old Testament, is "not idle" but active and impending.[58] Their impending destruction in hell is "not asleep." Peter personifies eternal damnation as if it were an executioner, who remains fully awake, ready to administer God's just sentence of condemnation on those who falsify his word.[59]

God is not sleeping, but is like a hunter following his prey, false teachers will be taken down. There is a judgment hanging over them. Truly damnation in hell waits for them from the Almighty God who pursues these false teachers with unsleeping eyes.

The Bible describes Christ coming in power and glory when the lost will be chased down by the wrath of God. Rebels both small and great run for their lives, but they cannot outrun the wrath of God.

> *Revelation 6:15-16* | Then the kings of the earth and the great ones and the generals and the rich and the powerful, and everyone, slave and free, hid themselves in the caves and among the rocks of the

---

[57] Ibid.
[58] Green, *2 Peter and Jude*, 120.
[59] MacArthur, *2 Peter and Jude*, 83–84.

mountains, ¹⁶ calling to the mountains and rocks, "Fall on us and hide us from the face of him who is seated on the throne, and from the wrath of the Lamb, ¹⁷ for the great day of their wrath has come, and who can stand?"

False teachers are think that they can outrun the wrath of God. They think they are safe in church under the sound of these false teachers. No church can protect us from the wrath of God. It is only the blood of Jesus that can shelter us from the wrath we deserve.

REMEMBER THEIR PAST (2:4-10)

God will not ignore false teachers, nor will he forget those who stand fast against them.[60]

To see how these false prophets operate, just look to their past. Be warned by their misery and perdition. Peter continues his denouncement of false teachers by referencing three well-known accounts of divine judgment from the book of Genesis.[61] In each case, these examples seemed to be flourishing, but judgement came down swiftly from the Lord.

These three representative and typological examples of God's judgment demonstrate that God's character has not changed. Previous judgments in history point toward and anticipate the final judgment, which is the climax of all other judgments.[62] There are three (or four if you count Lot) "if" statements about God's judgment, but the argument doesn't conclude until verse 9. Essentially Peter makes a very powerful argument:

> God rescues the righteous from false teachers. If God judged the unrighteous angels, rescued Noah while he judged the ancient sinful world in a flood, and rescued Lot while he judged wicked Sodom, then the Lord knows how to rescue the godly from the trials of false teachers that we face today.

Remember the Angels

Dear saints, God rescues the righteous from false teachers. He's got a bullseye of judgement on false teachers. They have transgressed just like the wicked fallen angels of old.

---

[60] Douglas Harink, 1 & 2 Peter (Grand Rapids, MI: Brazos Press, 2009), 99.
[61] MacArthur, *2 Peter and Jude*, 84.
[62] Schreiner, *1, 2 Peter, Jude*, 334.

The first story Peter talks about occurs in the *heavenly realm*. Peter tells us to remember the angels fell from their first estate, when they rebelled at creation (Eze 28:15) and one third of the angels fell from glory (Rev 12:4) and became demons. Or perhaps he may be referring to when fallen angels intermingled with women (*cf* Gen 6:1-4).[63]

The fallen angels are the great uncontrollable cosmic and historical beings whose rebel powers we see in the form of powerful ideals, all false religions, isms, worldviews, causes, movements. These wicked creatures lay hold of epochs, empires, peoples, nations, societies, institutions, and persons, and they enslave them, and make them serve systems of hostility, exploitation, destruction, war, and violence—the systems of sin and death. They are the "diverse manifestations of a seamless web of reality hostile to God" (1 Pet 3:18–22).[64] Make no mistake, Peter says, they have invited God's swift judgment.

> **2 Peter 2:4** | For if God did not spare angels when they sinned, but cast them into hell and committed them to chains of gloomy darkness to be kept until the judgment.

God judged the angels swiftly. If God did not even spare his angels, neither will he spare the false teachers. Judgment will come. Remember the specific judgment upon the angels.

The angels sinned. All the angels sinned and fell from grace. Remember the witness of Jesus.

> *Luke 10:18* | I saw Satan fall like lightning from heaven.

Some of the cosmic suprahuman powers (angels) rebel against the authority of God and their rightful role in the cosmic order.[65] Rather than serving God and God's purposes for his creatures, as they were created to do, these angels turn to serve themselves and to bend the minds, wills, and bodies of human beings to their own unrighteous ends. They become the "evil rulers and authorities of the unseen world,

---

[63] Bruce B. Barton, *1 & 2 Peter and Jude—Life Application Bible Commentary* (Carol Stream, IL: Tyndale, 1995), 165.

[64] Marva J. Dawn, *Powers, Weakness, and the Tabernacling of God* (Grand Rapids, MI: Wm. B. Eerdmans Publishing, 2001), 19.

[65] See John Howard Yoder, *The Politics of Jesus: Vicit Agnus Noster*, 2nd ed. (Grand Rapids: Eerdmans, 1994), 134–61; and Marva J. Dawn, *Powers, Weakness, and the Tabernacling of God* (Grand Rapids: Eerdmans, 2001).

... mighty powers in this dark world, and ... evil spirits in the heavenly places" (Eph. 6:12) who are opposed to God and his reign.

Some angels were confined. God conquered those powers through the cross of Christ.

> *Colossians 2:15* | He disarmed the rulers and authorities and put them to open shame, by triumphing over them in him [Christ].

The rebellious powers, Peter says, God confined some of them into hell—not the lake of fire, but the underworld (i.e., Tartarus—in Hellenistic thought, the place of divine punishment).[66] There are some demons who roam the earth, but many others are committed to "chains of gloomy darkness to be kept until the judgment." Some demons are already confined to Hades, the place where the lost go when they die, awaiting final judgment at the second coming of Christ.

Fallen angels will face final judgment. There is coming a day of final judgment for Satan, his angels, and the lost. Satan and his demons all know their time is short (Rev 12:12). That day of judgment is coming sooner rather than later. One day it will finally arrive.

> *Revelation 20:10-15* | The devil who had deceived them was thrown into the lake of fire and sulfur where the beast and the false prophet were, and they will be tormented day and night forever and ever. [11] Then I saw a great white throne and him who was seated on it. From his presence earth and sky fled away, and no place was found for them. [12] And I saw the dead, great and small, standing before the throne, and books were opened. Then another book was opened, which is the book of life. And the dead were judged by what was written in the books, according to what they had done. [13] And the sea gave up the dead who were in it, Death and Hades gave up the dead who were in them, and they were judged, each one of them, according to what they had done. [14] Then Death and Hades were thrown into the lake of fire. This is the second death, the lake of fire. [15] And if anyone's name was not found written in the book of life, he was thrown into the lake of fire.

If angels, who are a higher and stronger being than man cannot escape God's judgment, than what makes you think you can get away with following any false teacher?[67] Don't follow false prophets. They follow the devil and his angels. They are leading people to the pit of hell.

---

[66] Harink, *1 & 2 Peter*, 100.
[67] Mbuvi, *Jude and 2 Peter*, 74.

Jesus will separate the sheep from the goats on the Last Day, and he will say to the goats who think they know him, but are completely lost:

> Matthew 25:41 | Depart from me, you cursed, into the eternal fire prepared for the devil and his angels.

Remember the fallen angels. God put some of the angels in confinement. And those who now harass you have a judgment that is coming. Be assured that God will preserve you from their demonic harassment in the heavenly realm (Eph 6:10-13). Final judgment is coming for all the angels, the false teachers and the lost souls that follow them.

Remember the Ancient World

The next story Peter tells from Genesis takes place in the *earthly realm* of the ancient world where Noah and his family are the only righteous people left on earth. If God can rescue Noah in the midst of the wickedness of the ancient (Gen 6-8), he can rescue you! Don't give in to the false teachers.

> **2 Peter 2:5** | If he did not spare the ancient world, but preserved Noah, a herald of righteousness, with seven others, when he brought a flood upon the world of the ungodly.

Peter refers to the global flood three times in his two letters (*cf* 1 Pet 3:20; 2 Pet 2:5; 3:6). God's judgment is coming. It came so suddenly in Noah's day.

Noah's difficulty. How hard it must have been for Noah to live in the ancient world. He didn't belong there. He hated the wickedness. Yet God rescued and preserved him and his family. God did not spare the ancient world.

Noah's duty. Salvation had been available to all. Certainly, Noah, as a "herald of righteousness" was faithful to proclaim the way to God by grace through faith. However, few had chosen to believe. All those years Noah spent building the ark are a time of proclamation of the coming judgment, and of delayed judgment. Sadly, the people of Noah's day mocked him in their unbelief.

God destruction. "Flood" translates *kataklusmos*, from which the English *cataclysm* derives. The Genesis account, along with current geological evidence, indicates that the flood truly was *cataclysmic* in every sense (*cf* Gen 7:10–24).[68] Because of man's sinfulness, God destroyed every person and every land animal (except those in the ark), covering the entire planet with water—even the peaks of the highest mountains (Gen 7:19–20).[69]

Noah's deliverance. The great sinfulness of all mankind led the Lord to destroy the entire mass of humanity, sparing only the godly among them. Like then, judgment is coming today, this time not with water, but with fire. Yet because we as Christ followers know the Lord, there is nothing to fear in our own day of unbelief, since the Lord powerfully protected those who followed him, eight people in all: Noah and seven of his family (his wife, three sons, and their wives, Gen 8:16).

This is, as Peter says, the "world of the ungodly" (2 Pet. 2:5) that presses in upon Noah from all sides and ridicules the seeming irrationality of his faith in God's coming judgment and new creation as he builds a huge seaworthy boat in a dry land.

> *Hebrews 11:7* | By faith Noah, warned by God about events as yet unseen, respected the warning and built an ark to save his household; by this he condemned the world and became an heir to the righteousness that is in accordance with faith.

Noah was indeed a righteous man in his world, but he could not deliver himself from it. He stood firm and trusted God to rescue him from that corrupt world through the flood. But the flood did not wipe out the sinful inclination of the human heart itself, as God himself acknowledges (Gen. 8:21). The world of humankind, the very progeny of righteous Noah, remains the world of the ungodly, the world of sinners and enemies of God. Since God is not wishing that any should perish again in a flood, the worlds' violent and destructive evil inclination must be met with an even more radical act of God to deal with it: it requires the atoning and reconciling death of Jesus Christ (Rom 5:6–11), "the righteousness of our God and Savior Jesus Christ" (2 Pet 1:1) who delivers us "from the corruption that is in the world because of lust" (1:4).

God punishes the ungodly. His punishment is not arbitrary. Those who deserve punishment will receive his punishment; those who trust

---

[68] MacArthur, *2 Peter and Jude*, 88.
[69] See John C. Whitcomb, Jr., and Henry M. Morris, *The Genesis Flood* (Grand Rapids: Baker, 1961).

in him will receive his mercy and grace. As it was in Noah's day, it is today. God will destroy the ungodly and preserve anyone who comes to him by faith in his Son.[70] Remember the ancient world and flee from false teachers! Look how God spared Noah. He can rescue you from the ungodly as well.

Remember Sodom and Gomorrah

Peter's final story from Genesis takes place in the city or we might say the *political realm*—that sphere in which worship, history, culture, politics, economics, and social order might come together for the sake of the common good and human flourishing.[71] Yet in Lot's day, as today, the people worshipped the creation in place of the Creator—they loved the wrapping paper more than the gift as it were. It led them to unspeakable immorality. As believers, we live very uncomfortable lives in the earthly sphere, longing for the new creation where there is no sin or rebellion against God. I can't wait for that day. But like Lot, we are lured by the comforts of this world even while we are vexed by the world.

There in Sodom, Lot lived among the ungodly with his righteous soul afflicted day after day. God delivered Lot from the wickedness of Sodom and Gomorrah, and he can deliver you.

> **2 Peter 2:6-8** | If by turning the cities of Sodom and Gomorrah to ashes he condemned them to extinction, making them an example of what is going to happen to the ungodly. **7** And if he rescued righteous Lot, greatly distressed by the sensual conduct of the wicked **8** (for as that righteous man lived among them day after day, he was tormenting his righteous soul over their lawless deeds that he saw and heard).

The ruin of Sodom and Gomorrah. False teaching leads to false behavior and ultimately always produce suffering and disaster, be it in Lot's day, in Peter's, or in our own.[72] God condemned these infamous cities "to extinction," never to be inhabited again. These cities were "an

---

[70] Barton, *1 & 2 Peter and Jude*, 159.

[71] Bernd Wannenwetsch, "Representing the Absent in the City: Prolegomena to a Negative Political Theology according to Revelation 21," in *God, Truth, and Witness: Engaging Stanley Hauerwas*, ed. L. Gregory Jones, Reinhard Hütter, and C. Rosalee Velloso Ewell (Grand Rapids: Brazos, 2005), 167–192.

[72] Green, *2 Peter and Jude*, 123.

example of what is going to happen to the ungodly." All the cozy comfortable places that the wicked find shelter will also be condemned to extinction. All the nice houses and cars we see—the beautiful vacation spots—all the banks—all the sporting arenas—all of it will be "condemned to extinction" when the Lord comes again.

The reprobation of the ungodly. The destruction of Sodom and Gomorrah may seem extreme, but it's only a dress rehearsal for the great and frightening day of the Lord. These cities were merely "an example of what is going to happen to the ungodly" (vs 6). Christ will condemn the wicked to the lake of fire. The day is coming when the souls of the ungodly will receive the full vengeance of the living God.

> *2 Thessalonians 1:7-10* | When the Lord Jesus is revealed from heaven with his mighty angels [8] in flaming fire, inflicting vengeance on those who do not know God and on those who do not obey the gospel of our Lord Jesus. [9] They will suffer the punishment of eternal destruction, away from the presence of the Lord and from the glory of his might, [10] when he comes on that day to be glorified in his saints, and to be marveled at among all who have believed, because our testimony to you was believed.

The rescue of Lot. Daily, as he lived in these fertile but filthy cities, Lot's soul was vexed (KJV) and greatly distressed day after day as he saw the immoral conduct of the wicked. His righteous soul was tormented. Lot, righteous though he is, is not able to save himself. According to the Genesis story, he is a man also deeply attracted to the city—no doubt by its great power and beauty, its rich cultural and social life, and its economic wealth. So in the end Lot is unable to leave the city of his own will, even though it faces imminent destruction.[73]

Righteous Lot didn't want to relinquish his comfort and standing in society. Lot differs from Noah since Noah is a preacher of righteousness on the outskirts of the political realm. Noah lives a separated life from the world. Lot on the other hand is smackdab in the middle of the politic of his age. Because he is predestined for holiness (Rom 8:29), God does what lot is unwilling to do. He sends angels to drag him out of Sodom.

> *Genesis 19:15-16* | As morning dawned, the angels urged Lot, saying, "Up! Take your wife and your two daughters who are here, lest you be

---

[73] Harink, *1 & 2 Peter*, 100-101.

swept away in the punishment of the city." ¹⁶ But he lingered. So the men seized him and his wife and his two daughters by the hand, the Lord being merciful to him, and they brought him out and set him outside the city.

Can you imagine? God's angels urge Lot to leave, but "he lingered." So the angels had to seize Lot and his family. This was "the Lord being merciful to him." God is also merciful to us. If you do not leave your place of comfort, God will drag you from it. He delivered righteous Lot, and he will deliver you.

So the church and its members linger and hesitate and ask whether some realistic compromise might not be possible when we should flee unrighteousness and live for our heavenly city, living out our heavenly citizenship.

> *Philippians 3:20* | Our citizenship is in heaven, and from it we await a Savior, the Lord Jesus Christ,

Remember Judgment Day is Coming

Why all this remembering? Because the righteous and the wicked are on two cosmically different pathways. The pathway of the godly leads to mercy and rescue. The pathway of the unrighteous leads to punishment and judgment.

> **2 Peter 2:9-10a** | Then the Lord knows how to rescue the godly from trials, and to keep the unrighteous under punishment until the day of judgment, ¹⁰ and especially those who indulge in the lust of defiling passion and despise authority.

What does Judgment Day mean for the saints of God?

A Word for the Saints

> **2 Peter 2:9a** | Then the Lord knows how to rescue the godly from trials.

The Lord will rescue the saints from their trials and suffering. Peter insists that God's coming judgment will not sweep up the righteous with the wicked. Because God is just, He will spare the righteous believers in Christ, rescuing them from coming judgment.[74]

---

[74] Swindoll, *Insights on James and 1 & 2 Peter*, 295.

You may have attacks from the *heavenly realm* by the fallen angels who influence the false prophets. You may have attacks from the *earthly realm* because you are living separated from the world. Even if you have fallen like Lot in the *cultural realm* and succumbed to the comfort of this world, the Lord will rescue the true believer. But the wicked stand condemned, awaiting future wrath.

A Word for Sinners

2 Peter 2:9b | And to keep the unrighteous under punishment until the day of judgment.

The lost are "under punishment" awaiting their final judgment. They cannot escape. Their case has already been referred to the divine Supreme Court to be taken up on the day of judgment.[75] What is the punishment that the lost are suffering while awaiting the day of judgment? The unrighteous are like prisoners in jail who await final sentencing and transfer to their final fate.[76]

First, the lost are "under punishment" because their life is under the power and harassment of the devil. Those who are lost live empty lives in regard to eternity, yet their lives are nonetheless filled with lots of things, bad things, like the demonic harassment of anger, anxiety, and the idolatry of lust and empty, worldly pleasures. The lost are constantly harassed by the god of this world, Satan and his minions.

2 *Corinthians 4:4* | The god of this world has blinded the minds of the unbelievers, to keep them from seeing the light of the gospel of the glory of Christ, who is the image of God.

Second, the lost are "under punishment" because while they wait, they continue to accumulate more guilt (*cf* Rom 2:3–6). The guilt of the heart must be cleansed by the blood of Christ, but the lost live without this mercy. They are harassed by their own bad choices with no remedy for their guilt. They drown out the noise of their conscience through drink and substance, through mindless entertainment, through short-lived relationships. They will try to fill the eternal void in their heart that only the one true God can fill.

---

[75] John Phillips, *Exploring the Epistles of Peter: An Expository Commentary*, The John Phillips Commentary Series (Kregel Publications; WORDsearch Corp., 2009), 2 Pe 2:9.

[76] MacArthur, *2 Peter and Jude*, 92.

A Word for Scoffers

2 Peter 2:10a | And especially those who indulge in the lust of defiling passion and despise authority.

Peter brings the discussion full circle, again recounting the false teachers' two primary characteristics. They scoff at holiness and accountability. Peter says that judgment is "especially" reserved for scoffers who know the truth but sin in the light. Most sin in the darkness, not knowing the word of God and have not clearly heard of the love of our Savior. But there are those in the pulpits and pews who are sinning not in the darkness, but in the broad daylight. They are especially guilty of the greatest condemnation and the darkest and deepest part of hell with its bottomless pit and lake of fire.

They are always hiding their sin under the cover of "grace" and a flimsy sort of righteous religiosity. Christ wants to puke such people out of his mouth (Rev 3:16). Though they preach, cast out demons, and see miracle occur, they have no part in the body of Christ, because they are devoid of inward holiness (*cf* Mt 7:21-23). The righteous, on the other hand are constantly dragging their sin into the light, confessing their sins to one another, and bearing each other's burdens.

> *Proverbs 28:13* | Whoever conceals his transgressions will not prosper, but he who confesses and forsakes them will obtain mercy.

Let me ask you, are you participating in anything illicit or immoral? Are you indulging in pornography? Drunkenness? Are you popping pills or taking other substances to numb yourself? Do not rest in your Bible knowledge. The true faith of those who are born again have the power to live holy lives. If you are a true believer, you will stop the immorality. You will stop the substance and the drunkenness, and you will, right now, renew your covenant with Christ. Don't be coy, scoffing at holiness. Be sober and listen to the words of Paul to the Ephesians.

> *Ephesians 5:5-6, 11* | You may be sure of this, that everyone who is sexually immoral or impure, or who is covetous (that is, an idolater), has no inheritance in the kingdom of Christ and God. ⁶ Let no one deceive you with empty words, for because of these things the wrath of God comes upon the sons of disobedience.... ¹¹ Take no part in the unfruitful works of darkness, but instead expose them.

Again, Paul warns the Corinthians that no immoral person, nor anyone who is willing to live under the power and control of alcohol or drugs has any inheritance in the kingdom of God (1 Cor 6:9-10). The righteous tremble at these warnings. The wicked will scoff and disregard them.

Psalm 1 tells us that the blessed man does not "sin in the seat of scoffers," but "his delight is in the law of the Lord ... day and night," and he is "like a tree planted by the rivers of water," being very fruitful (Psa 1:1-3). Remember the conclusion of the Psalm.

> Psalm 1:6 | The LORD knows the way of the righteous, but the way of the wicked will perish.

Judgment is coming. Scoffing at it is very fashionable today, but it God will not delay. Flee to Christ or face unavoidable judgment.

Conclusion

Dear saints, don't be fooled by false preachers. They only desire followers so they can fleece them. They feed their own lusts. They do not spare the flock, but only protect themselves. They are cowards, and their judgment is certain and imminent. What can we do? What can anyone do? Flee to Christ.

It reminds me of the story of the pioneers who went west on the Oregon Trail. They traveled in covered wagons. Progress was unusually slow. One day they found out why. A wildfire was raging, stretching for miles across the prairie, coming toward them rapidly. One man only seemed to understand what could be done. He gave the command to set fire to the grass behind them. Then when a space was burned over, the whole company moved back upon it.

As the flames roared on toward them from the west, a little girl cried out in terror, "Are you sure we shall not all be burned up?"

The leader replied, "My child, the flames cannot reach us here, for we are standing where the fire has been!"

What a picture of the believer, who is safe in Christ! The only safe place from the judgment of God is in the one who has already received judgment: in Christ alone.[77]

---

[77] H.A. Ironside, *Illustrations of Bible Truth* (Chicago: Moody Press, 1945), 34-35.

6 | 2 PETER 2:10b-22

HOW TO SPOT A COUNTERFEIT

For if, after they have escaped the defilements of the world through the knowledge of our Lord and Savior Jesus Christ, they are again entangled in them and overcome, the last state has become worse for them than the first.

2 PETER 2:20

Have you ever heard of identity theft? Forty-nine percent of Americans experienced financial identity theft in 2020.[78] This means, somebody who you don't know opens up new accounts in your name and spends your money and your reputation as if they were really you. Identity theft costs $56 billion dollars and 300 million hours in lost time annually for these people.[79] There's another kind of identity theft going on. People who call themselves Christians but still love the world. There are even false pastors and prophets among us that claim to know the Lord, teach the word with accuracy, but actually are

---

[78] Federal Trade Commission, *Facts + Statistics: Identity Theft and Cybercrime* (Washington DC: Consumer Sentinel Network, 2022), Retrieved June 2, 2022, from https://www.iii.org/fact-statistic/facts-statistics-identity-theft-and-cybercrime

[79] Megan Leonhardt, *Consumers Lost $56 Billion to Identity Fraud Last Year-Here's What To Look Out For* (New York: CNBC, 2021, March 23). Retrieved June 2, 2022, from https://www.cnbc.com/2021/03/23/consumers-lost-56-billion-dollars-to-identity-fraud-last-year.html

children of the devil. These are the devil's most dangerous weapons because they are so disillusioning.

We need to be able to spot a counterfeit teacher. Good pastors and elders are going to drag the counterfeit under the light and expose false teachers. Faithful shepherds protect their sheep. They work hard, day after day, to instruct, reprove, correct, and train God's people (*cf* 2 Tim 3:16–17)—leading their flocks on the path of truth (Psa 119:105). Like the Good Shepherd himself, they stand guard even when spiritual enemies threaten (Acts 20:28–32; *cf* Jn 10:13–14). Cowardice is not a consideration for them; neither is compromise. After all, they have received a divine commission, to "shepherd the flock of God until the Chief Shepherd appears" (1 Pet 5:2, 4).[80] So let's examine the characteristics of false teachers.

FALSE TEACHERS ARE ARROGANT (2:10B-11)

There is nothing more offensive to God than the distortion of his word (*cf* Rev 22:18–19). To falsify the facts about who God is and what he said—even promoting Satan's lies as if they were God's truth—is the basest form of hypocrisy. With eternity at stake, it is hard to believe that anyone would intentionally deceive other people, teaching them something that is spiritually catastrophic. Yet, such is the atrocious arrogance of false prophets.[81] The willingness to twist God's word begins in their character.

Arrogant in Their Character

2 Peter 2:10b | Bold and willful.

Ever since Satan's initial rebellion (*cf* Eze 28:17), pride has been the primary characteristic of God's enemies (*cf* 1 Tim. 3:6).[82] False teachers have hardened their conscience. They excuse their sin and make excuses for themselves in the most bold and willful ways. Their boldness smacks of the reckless daring that defies God and man. Their willfulness describes someone determined to please himself at all costs.[83] False teachers often surround themselves in such a way as to avoid accountability.

---

[80] MacArthur, *2 Peter and Jude*, 96.
[81] Ibid., 67.
[82] Ibid., 97.
[83] Green, *2 Peter and Jude*, 127.

Arrogant in Their Contempt

Many false teachers ignore or mock the unseen realm and blaspheme the angelic realm by dismissing it and not taking it seriously.

> **2 Peter 2:10c-11** | They do not tremble as they blaspheme the glorious ones, [11] whereas angels, though greater in might and power, do not pronounce a blasphemous judgment against them before the Lord.

The "glorious ones" in this context refers to demons (*cf* Jude 8), who are distinct from humanity in that they are transcendent, supernatural beings, beyond the human level (Eph 6:12).[84] False teachers mostly dismiss or ignore these beings and help people feel comfortable in their cultural, materialistic, worldly context. They are glad to embrace the popular dogmas of their secular age, like the theistic evolutionists of so many churches of liberalism today. They would rather preach psychology with just a small dab of Bible words here and there. They teach enough of the Bible to inoculate their hearers. Archibald Brown, a student of Charles Spurgeon, said it well.

> A time will come when instead of shepherds feeding the sheep, the church will have clowns entertaining the goats! [85]

Providing amusement for the people is nowhere spoken of in Scripture as a function of the church. We are to be the salt of the earth, not sugar-coated candy. We do not gather to entertain our kids or to entertain each other. We are here to see the serious work of Holy Spirit anointing and holiness as he applies the word of God with authority to our lives.

It reminds me of the twentieth-century novel *The Flight of Peter Fromm*. The book traces the disheartening journey of one young man, Peter Fromm, who recreates and edits the gospel, so as not to offend his hearers. His goal, like so many false teachers, is "to preach without saying anything."[86]

---

[84] MacArthur, *2 Peter and Jude*, 98.

[85] Archibald Geikie Brown, *The Devil's Mission of Amusement: A Protest* (London: Morgan & Scott, 1889). See chapter on "Amusing the Goats or Feeding the Sheep." Online: https://banneroftruth.org/us/resources/articles/2002/feeding-sheep-or-amusing-goats/

[86] Helm, *1 & 2 Peter and Jude*, 231.

To be a minister today in the typical church of a prosperous suburb, one must be as skilled as a politician in the rhetoric of ambiguity, circumlocution, and doubletalk. He must talk plain language though in such a way that no listener can take offense. He may attack race prejudice, but it must be done obliquely so that no one in the congregation imagines that it refers to him. He may attack business ethics, but it must be done in such a manner that no businessman who listens will think that he is implicated. Today's preacher can indeed use all doctrinal phrases but always so cunningly that conservative listeners will take them one way, liberal listeners another. In brief he must learn to preach without saying anything.[87]

Many in our world are in love with the culture, the here and now, the non-supernatural. They love what they can see with their eyes and mock the supernatural. They ignore and even deny the reality of the spiritual world and claim that only what can be seen and felt is real.

They teach a kind of "moral therapeutic deism" where God is a kind of distant force that wants you to live morally and peacefully. He wants you to be respectful. No need for a Savior. No need for the supernatural. False teachers are big into this. As long as you "live your best life now." It's kind of a teaching of self-esteem and respectfulness. There is no need for repentance of sin or the cross of Christ.[88]

Like the false teachers of Peter's day, these false teachers are fools who will be proven wrong in the end. Don't take Satan and his supernatural evil powers lightly. Although Satan will be destroyed completely, he is at work now trying to render Christians complacent and ineffective.[89]

FALSE TEACHERS ARE ADULTEROUS (2:12-16)

Peter summarizes the life and attitude of false teachers: they have "eyes full of adultery" (2:14). They are unfaithful in all they do. They say they belong to the "Master who bought them" (2:1), but in their heart they are dedicated to another.

---

[87] Marvin Gardiner, *The Flight of Peter Fromm* (Amherst, MA: Prometheus Books, 1994), 9.

[88] Christian Smith and Melinda Lundquist Denton, *Soul Searching: The Religious and Spiritual Lives of American Teenagers* (Oxford, UK: Oxford University Press, 2009), 162–164.

[89] Barton, *1 & 2 Peter and Jude,* 165.

Unfaithful in Their Teaching: They Falsify

"They promise them freedom" (2:19). The false teachers claim the gospel has set the believer free from the need to follow moral rules.[90] What falsehood. They don't have the Spirit to guide them, so they follow their flesh. Every choice for sin and rebellion is a slide away from the image of God and a giant leap toward an animalistic, base nature of beasts. This so-called "freedom" is really slavery.

> 2 Peter 2:12a | But these, like irrational animals, creatures of instinct, born to be caught and destroyed, blaspheming about matters of which they are ignorant.

Their description. Peter describes these false teachers as "irrational animals" who have chosen sin to have also chosen to slowly lose the image of God in them. This being so, their behavior sinks to the level of mere animal instinct. As so often happens with people who think themselves above the need to yield to moral rules, their freedom means, in practice, a life devoted to sensual self-indulgence, like a hungry animal following his base appetite.[91] Remember that God created appetites for food and pleasure and enjoyment of life, but only when Christ is at the center can true freedom be experienced. Without Christ, these blessings of God become the slave masters of our lives.

Their destiny. These false teachers, like animals, are "born to be caught and destroyed." Such harsh words reveal the seriousness of the false teachers' sin. Those who teach have great responsibility. Jesus has very harsh words for those false teachers who would try and deceive his children.

> Mark 9:42 | Whoever causes one of these little ones who believe in me to sin, it would be better for him if a great millstone were hung around his neck and he were thrown into the sea.

Teachers who lead others astray will face great punishment. False teachers set aside self-restraint in order to follow their passions and numb their conscience and awareness of the judgment that's coming. Like animals, unaware that they are likely to be hunted and slaughtered, the false teachers can't see the eternal danger of their

---

[90] Richard J. Bauckham, *2 Peter–Jude*, ed. David A. Hubbard and Ralph P. Martin, Word Biblical Themes (Grand Rapids, MI: Zondervan Academic, 1990), 67.
[91] Ibid., 69.

immorality. Thus, false teachers who think their teaching is superior to the outdated and unfashionable word of God actually have the intellect of animals who are unable to reason.[92]

False teachers are so hardened they act more like animals who can't see the trapper instead of those made in God's image. The picture is that of predatory animals which men deliberately catch or snare in order to destroy. Such is the destiny of men who act like wild and savage beasts. Sensuality is self-destructive.[93] God will trap them like a vicious animal, and there will be no escape.

Their doctrine. These false teachers are "blaspheming about matters of which they are ignorant." This is an interesting insight. Peter is essentially saying that the false teachers may say true things about God and his glory, but because they are God's enemies, they have no place talking about God's glory and majesty and are actually blaspheming his name. When reprobates speak of "the glories" of Christ as well as "many holy things, of which these heretics in reality know nothing," they are actually blaspheming.[94] Some false teachers are easy to spot—they twist the person and work of Christ by teaching a works salvation of legalism, or a cheap grace salvation of license. Others use orthodox teaching as a cover for their licentious living.

Their deficiency. These false teachers are ignorant of the power and pleasure of the Holy Spirit. These counterfeit Christians who criticize the heart of holiness and the joy in chastity and moral uprightness have never experienced the true freedom of the Holy Spirit, and the "fullness of joy" that is at God's "right hand" of his presence "forevermore" (Psa 16:11). For the one submitted to the Spirit, the glory of our pleasure in God far outweighs the suffering and trials of the Christian life (Rom 8:18).

> *2 Corinthians 4:17* | This light momentary affliction is preparing for us an eternal weight of glory beyond all comparison.

---

[92] Ibid., 68.
[93] Hiebert, *Second Peter and Jude,* 114.
[94] R. C. H. Lenski, *The Interpretation of the Epistles of St. Peter, St. John and St. Jude* (Minneapolis: Augsburg, 1961), 327.

Unfaithful in Their Promises: They Flatter

The false teachers promise carnal pleasure now and in the hereafter, but their promises are false. They flatter their hearers, giving them false assurance, all the while, they are headed for destruction.

> **2 Peter 2:12b-13a** | But these... will also be destroyed in their destruction, **13** suffering wrong as the wage for their wrongdoing.

The false teachers have done enormous harm and will be treated accordingly. In the end, false teachers fall victims to their own propaganda and believe their own lies. As a result, they succumb to the consequences of their corrupt lifestyles, which is destruction in hell forever.[95] Peter has a play on words here. *The wage for taking other people's wages is destruction.* The wages of sin, indeed, is death (Rom 6:23a). They will receive harm for the harm they have done (*cf* 2:13a). They will reap exactly what they have sown (Gal 6:7). False teachers live the high life, but only for a moment.

> *Hebrews 9:7* | It is appointed for man to die once, and after that comes judgment.

Keep in mind when you hear false teachers, they cannot deliver what they promise. They promise hedonism on earth and grace in the life to come, but they cannot deliver. Sin catches up to you at the end. If there is no repentance in life, there is rarely repentance on the deathbed. The wages of your corruption now will catch up to you, because you are part of the ultimate statistic. Ten out of ten people die. It reminds me of the last letter the infamous atheist, Voltaire, ever wrote:

> I, the underwritten, do declare that for these four days past, having been afflicted with vomiting of blood—at the age of 84—and not being able to drag myself to church, the reverend having been pleased to add to his many favors that of sending me Father Gautier, I did confess to him, that if it please God to dispose of me, I would die in the Church in which I was born. Hoping that the divine mercy will pardon my faults, I sign myself below,
>
> François-Marie d'Arouet Voltaire, March 2, 1778[96]

---

[95] Phillips, *Exploring the Epistles of Peter*, 2 Pe 2:12–13a.
[96] François-Marie Arouet Voltaire in David James Burrell, *The Morning Cometh: Talks for the Times* (New York: American Tract Society, 1893), 133.

But reconciliation with the *Church* is not reconciliation with *Christ*. It is said that he died with such shrieks and blasphemies on his lips as to drive the nurses and doctors from the room.

Unfaithful in Their Dignity: They are Fools

These false teachers have no dignity.

> **2 Peter 2:13b** | They count it pleasure to revel in the daytime.

As a general rule, sinners tend to engage in debauchery at night: "For those who sleep do their sleeping at night, and those who get drunk get drunk at night" (1 Thess 5:7). According to historians, even the pagan Roman society tolerated dissipation and revelry as long as it was discreetly confined to the cover of darkness. Nonetheless, the false teachers of Peter's day were so consumed with lust, greed, and vice that they considered it a "pleasure to revel in the daytime," not wanting to wait until nightfall.[97]

As a tree is known by its fruit, so the actions of false teachers expose their corrupt nature (Mt 7:18–20). As the list of their vices shows, false doctrine inevitably produces immoral living.[98] We grow in holiness and love for truth because of the indwelling Christ within us by the Holy Spirit. Because these false teachers have rejected the pleasures of heaven, they revel in the pleasures of the underworld here on earth.

Unfaithful in Their Integrity: They Fabricate

> **2 Peter 2:13c** | They are blots and blemishes, reveling in their deceptions, while they feast with you.

In light of their passion for perversion, Peter likened these spiritual charlatans to "stains" and "blemishes"—two terms that speak of filthy spots, defects, scabs, and things diseased. Like malignant sores, the false teachers were reveling in their deceptions and openly enjoying the fruit of their sin. At the same time, they reveling in their deception by actively promoting wickedness in the lives of their followers.[99] Paul gave a powerful warning about these false teachers to the church at Rome.

---

[97] MacArthur, *2 Peter and Jude*, 100.
[98] Dieudonné Tamfu, *2 Peter and Jude* (Carlisle, UK: HippoBooks, 2018), 37.
[99] MacArthur, *2 Peter and Jude*, 100.

Romans 16:18 | Such persons do not serve our Lord Christ, but their own appetites, and by smooth talk and flattery they deceive the hearts of the naive.

Like a cancer, they overtake naïve people willing to believe their lies. People like Benny Hinn, Paula White, T.D. Jakes, Joel Osteen, and Kenneth Copeland are a few of the big-name false teachers of the early twenty-first century, but there will be many more to come. They love to sell, sell, sell. They love to take offerings. They love to fly around the country in their gold-plated jets. But they do not shepherd the sheep.

Paul says false teachers will deceive all the while they are feasting and partaking of the Lord's table with you. By feigning faith in Christ, the false teachers pretended to have a rightful place at the communion table. But in fact, they were a polluting influence.[100] Churches and pastors need to drag the arrogant lies and filthy lives of these false teachers into the light. The world's media has done exposes on some of these false teachers. But the church needs to expose the wolves. We need to name names and warn the sheep. We cannot allow them to hold sway whether in communion or in our own hearts by listening to their teaching. Turn them off. Avoid them. Warn and teach those around you to flee from their false teachings and wicked lives.

Unfaithful in Their Morality: They Fornicate

Many false teachers love the church format because they are predators. Like cruel animals, they do not spare the sheep. Peter warns us about these vicious wolves.

2 Peter 2:14a | They have eyes full of adultery, insatiable for sin. They entice unsteady souls.

We've mentioned some of the big-name wolves, but there are many tens of thousands more pastors and church leaders who are living not just extravagant lives, but filthy immoral lives. I used to hear about it when I would travel from church to church. I would sometimes hear: "My pastor has sinned in immorality. What should I do?" Dear little sheep of God, you need to flee a church like that unless they bring discipline upon that pastor. Pastors have to be held to account. Often these are false teachers—wolves in sheep's clothing who avoid accountability

---

[100] Ibid.

and simply go to another church. Often these false teachers are predators, and they need to be exposed!

> *Jude 1:4* | Certain people have crept in unnoticed who long ago were designated for this condemnation, ungodly people, who pervert the grace of our God into sensuality and deny our only Master and Lord, Jesus Christ.

Indeed, they say they are children of God, but they are as Peter says, "accursed children." And they are not children of God but they are of their father the devil, the father of lies.

Unfaithful in Their Finances: They Fleece

At the end of the day, false teachers love money. They are so far gone, even the rebuke of donkey wouldn't help them.

Their Financial Workout

2 Peter 2:14b | They have hearts trained in greed. Accursed children!

Peter says they have "hearts trained in greed." The word there that is translated *trained* is the word we get our word *gymnasium* from. And what is a gymnasium? It's a place where you go to train. And he says these people do constant reps and workouts in art of covetousness and greed. They want money. They want possessions. They want power. Now money and possession and power are not wrong when they are used for God. But when they're the root and the fruit of the flesh, when they are what motivates a person, rather than the glory of God, God says they are *"accursed children."* What does that mean? It means they are destined for divine destruction.[101] Their financial workout is in vain. Consider the piercing question that Jesus asks to those whose main purpose in life is to gain riches.

> *Mark 8:36-37* | What does it profit a man to gain the whole world and forfeit his soul? [37] For what can a man give in return for his soul?

The answer is you can give nothing that's of more value than your soul. Remember hell has no exits. Once there, you are there forever. We will all live forever somewhere. Don't follow the false teachers who are the accursed children of hell.

---

[101] Adrian Rogers, "Three Marks of an Apostate," in *Adrian Rogers Sermon Archive* (Signal Hill, CA: Rogers Family Trust, 2017), 2 Pe 2:9–16.

Their Financial Worthlessness

Where does their love for money bring them? To apostasy. They are worthless.

2 Peter 2:14c-15a | Accursed children! **15** Forsaking the right way, they have gone astray.

What is an apostate? An apostate is one who has known the way of truth, but never been saved, turned from the way of truth, and his latter end is worse than his first, which is exactly what Peter later says (2:20-21).

Their Financial Weakness

False teachers all have their price. They will compromise for a bit of money, just like the Old Testament false prophet, Balaam.

2 Peter 2:15b-16 | They have followed the way of Balaam, the son of Beor, who loved gain from wrongdoing, **16** but was rebuked for his own transgression; a speechless donkey spoke with human voice and restrained the prophet's madness.

Compromised by a foreign agent. Balaam acted as hired agent for the heathen king, Balak. These false teachers who seduced Christians acted as hired agents of a foreign employer.[102] False teachers are the hired hands of Satan himself.

Compromised by a filthy money. Every modern-day Balaam has his or her price. They may appear on the outside to be in it for the ministry, but it doesn't take long to realize they're in it for the money. And when the price is right, make no mistake, they exchange principle for profit.

This reminds me of the story of a crooked bank officer who approached a junior clerk and whispered to him one quiet afternoon, "Hey, if I gave you $25,000, would you help me, well, let's just say 'fix' the books? You know, make a few lucrative adjustments?"

The clerk responded, "Yeah, I suppose I could do that for $25,000."

His boss leaned in. "Would you do it for $100?"

Insulted, the clerk replied, "No way! What do you think I am? A common thief?"

---

[102] Green, *2 Peter and Jude*, 135.

The bank officer answered, "We've already established that. Now we're just negotiating the price."

The point of this story is that every fake has a price. Those who lack integrity will do anything to feed the greed.[103] False teachers get used to a comfortable lifestyle. "Their god is their belly" so they are willing to sacrifice integrity and morality for security and pleasure.

Compromised by a financial madness. Religious teachers motivated by greed will preach what people want to hear. Balaam was so crazy in love with money, he had to be rebuked by a talking donkey!

The love of money corrupts the heart. It is the root of all kinds of evil and is especially dangerous among the false and fashionable preachers. They don't mind tailoring their message for this world's comfort. This is the centerpiece of many a false gospel. False teachers are willing to relax the rigor of the gospel if you will let them fleece you. They live loose, preaching the word, but not applying it. Self-indulgence in the pulpit leads to self-indulgence in the pew. In order to support their pleasure-seeking lifestyle, they encourage a similar lifestyle among their disciples. They, and their followers, became slaves of mutually dependent self-interest. So much for their supposed freedom (*cf* 2:19)![104]

In the end, a dumb donkey possessed sounder prophetic vision than a religious official whose moral sense had been perverted by gain from wrongdoing[105]

FALSE TEACHERS ARE ABANDONED (2:17-22)

They speak of Jesus and call him Lord, but they deny the Master that bought them. They preach and do miracles and say they know Christ, but he does not know them. On the last day when Jesus is revealed in all his power and glory, these false teachers will hear the devasting words, "Depart from me, I never knew you" (Mt 7:23). Anyone can say they know Jesus, but the real question is: does Jesus know you? False teachers will ultimately be abandoned by the living God because they do not belong to him, but they belong to their father the devil.

---

[103] Swindoll, *Insights on James and 1 & 2 Peter*, 302.
[104] Bauckham, *2 Peter–Jude*, 69.
[105] Green, *2 Peter and Jude*, 136.

Abandoned to a Fruitless Destiny

False teachers are so deceiving. They emphasize prosperity in order to support their own luxurious way of life. They look so good, fruitful and successful on the outside, but they actually have no kingdom fruit to speak of. False teachers may have massive campaigns and television programs with fancy houses and jets. Yet they have no eternal fruit.

2 Peter 2:17a | These are waterless springs and mists driven by a storm.

After revealing the attack of the false teachers to fleece the sheep, he returns the attack and drags them into the broad daylight to uncover their true nature. Peter uses two brilliant metaphors: a waterless spring and a dry windstorm.

A Waterless Spring

Imagine the excitement. You see in the distance a glorious spring in the desert expecting fountains of water of refreshment, only to investigate and find it has no water! There are many promises and trappings and an impressive show of entertainment with false teachers, but they are unwilling to do teach and apply the truth in a way that requires them to get involved in the life of the sheep. They are merely hirelings and leave the sheep to their sins with no care to rescue them. They deceive the goats with a false gospel and leave them unregenerated, dead in their trespasses and sins. They lead the synagogues of Satan. The sheep are starving; the goats are unconverted. They preach no message that will transform the people. They are like emaciated souls stranded in a desert with a waterless well. We think here of Jeremiah's warning.

Jeremiah 2:13 | They have forsaken me, the spring of living water, and have dug their own cisterns, broken cisterns that cannot hold water.

It is only the man in touch with Christ, the water of life (Jn 4:13–14), who will find lasting satisfaction, and, indeed, will pour out of his inner being water that will satisfy the thirsty (Jn 7:38). Heterodoxy, psychology, and self-help are all very novel in the classroom; it is extremely unsatisfying in the heart and life.[106]

---

[106] Ibid., 137.

A Sand Storm

Peter uses a second illustrative metaphor: "mists driven by a storm," i.e., a sandstorm. A mist promises rain. Farmers need rain; the ground needs soaking. But these false preachers deliver nothing more than a passing haze.[107] False teachers are great at turning a phrase. They are masters of momentary inspiration. But like a storm coming after a drought, they can excite their hearers. The problem is, it turns out to be a dust storm. It brings no satisfaction but only misery. Such false teachers do not give real help to struggling marriages. Broken people remain broken. Instead of the sweet storm waters to satisfy the ground, they get battered by a message that is superficial and subversive to their walk with God. What heartbreak so many have in false churches today who long for their souls to be soaked only to get battered by the sand of psychology and a message that cannot transform or save.

Peter's point is that these false teachers are abandoned to fruitlessness. They cannot bring a message that brings relief, change, and meaningful transformation.

Change is not possible with gimmicks and mere self-effort. It is not possible with momentary inspiration. We need the heaven-sent dove to rest upon us. Only a message that not only demands repentance and holiness, but that comes with the infinite power of the Holy Spirit will do. We need showers of blessing. God can plant us near streams of living water. He can make us his mighty oaks of righteousness.

Abandoned to Forever Destruction

The warning for preachers, me included, is immense. Any of us who abandon the apostolic way, promote sensuality, and seek our own gain are springs that can't produce water; we are vapors that drift past the spiritually indigent like a haze. The end for any of us who conduct our ministry in such a lifeless way is haunting: the gloom of hell itself is reserved.[108]

> **2 Peter 2:17b** | For them the gloom of utter darkness has been reserved.

---

[107] Helm, *1 & 2 Peter and Jude*, 236.
[108] Ibid., 237.

False teachers claim to lead people into the light through their "enlightening" teachings, but they and those who follow all end up in the same place: "the gloom of utter darkness."[109]

The descriptions of hell describe a place of conscious suffering. It does not say these souls cease to exist, but that they will experience the terror and gloom of darkness. Why is there terror and gloom in the dark? You don't know what's happening. Hell, Peter says, is like an eternal dust storm. You get false doctrine in this life, it will abandon you blindness in this life and in the life to come.

Abandoned to Foolish Desire

The fear of the Lord (acknowledging him, and trembling before his presence) is the beginning of wisdom. False teachers may know the Bible, but they do not fear God. They not only live foolishly in immorality and carnal pleasure, they boast of their folly!

> **2 Peter 2:18** | For, speaking loud boasts of folly, they entice by sensual passions of the flesh those who are barely escaping from those who live in error. **19** They promise them freedom, but they themselves are slaves of corruption. For whatever overcomes a person, to that he is enslaved.

"Live free," these purveyors of carnality preach. They preach about liberty when all the time they themselves have been (and still are) in the prison-house of lust.[110] They forget the words of Jesus who said that whoever sins is a slave of sin. Freedom has never come by "doing what you want." That's the definition of being enslaved to carnal desire. To be truly free, one must be filled by the Spirit. You can only be free from carnal desire if you fill yourself with a new and more powerful desire: the love of God and the filling of the Holy Spirit. But the false teachers won't tell you that. One preacher in the early church who hated false teaching was Irenaeus. He grew up in Polycarp's church in Smyrna before being sent to Rome, then to Lyons in modern-day France. Throughout his life he encountered numerous false teachers.[111] He wrote a five-volume series against false teachers. Listen to his warning.

---

[109] Swindoll, *Insights on James and 1 & 2 Peter*, 302.
[110] Green, *2 Peter and Jude*, 140.
[111] Swindoll, *Insights on James and 1 & 2 Peter*, 302–305.

Error, indeed, is never set forth in its naked deformity, lest, being thus exposed, it should at once be detected. But it is craftily decked out in an attractive dress, so as, by its outward form, to make it appear to the inexperienced (ridiculous as the expression may seem) more true than the truth itself.[112]

Peter notes that there are perhaps some true believers in the midst of false congregations who are being enticed. He says they are "barely escaping those who are living in error." Peter is not writing theoretically about false teachers "far, far away" but to people he knows are being affected by them right now.

Perhaps you have also allowed yourself to be enticed by sexual sin. Maybe you have comforted yourself with the same lies of these false teachers. "God is a God of grace," you say. "He'll understand and forgive," you say to yourself. You may be a believer, but you are twisting the word of God. You are "barely escaping" those who have denied God. But you are not far away from God giving you over to that sin. Whoever truly belongs to God, he will not just look away from your sin. He will chastise his own children. You may be playing with sexual sin to the detriment of your own future. Perhaps you are putting your own marriage and family at risk. If you continue, you may lose your spouse. Your kids may lose the joy of seeing their daddy every day. God could take things away from you and give you over to Satan for a time to be chastened by illness or even death. Choosing sin today may means Satanic harassment with anxiety and despair and bitterness. Stop lying to yourself. No true Christian barely escapes for any significant period of time without great suffering. Chastening and misery and heartbreaking grief is always accompanied by the choice of a Christian to sin.

Every Christian has the power not to sin, but the wicked are abandoned to their own enslaving desires. False teachers boast in this filth. They will preach Song of Solomon like a slutty romance novel. They entice people with the false gospel of license. Flee from sexual sin and those who boast in it.

---

[112] Irenaeus of Lyons, *Against Heresies* 1.1.2, in *The Ante-Nicene Fathers: Translations of the Writings of the Fathers down to AD 325*, ed. Alexander Roberts et al.; vol. 1, *The Apostolic Fathers, Justin Martyr, Irenaeus*, American reprint ed. (New York: Charles Scribner's Sons, 1899), 315.

Abandoned Futile Damnation

No matter what the false teacher does, he or she cannot repent. They are given over to their own lies.

> **2 Peter 2:20-22** | For if, after they have escaped the defilements of the world through the knowledge of our Lord and Savior Jesus Christ, they are again entangled in them and overcome, the last state has become worse for them than the first. **21** For it would have been better for them never to have known the way of righteousness than after knowing it to turn back from the holy commandment delivered to them. **22** What the true proverb says has happened to them: "The dog returns to its own vomit, and the sow, after washing herself, returns to wallow in the mire."

These false teachers, in Peter's view, at one time preached the true gospel of Christ. There seemed to be some fruit, but they fall away. Likely Peter is referring to Jesus' parable of the false converts. There are some stony-ground hearers and thorny-ground hearers who escape the defilements of the world. They have freedom from their lusts and addictions for a time, but they have not fully surrendered to Christ in faith. They have a superficial faith. They have just added Jesus to their list of idols.

Those who only come to Christ superficially and then try to defend themselves, as if they have true faith, are in the worst position possible. It's one thing to sin in the darkness, not knowing the gospel. But false teachers sin in the light.

Peter, the fisherman, has a colorful imagination and relates those who know and even preach the gospel but then not live in the power of gospel holiness as dogs who eat their own vomit and cleaned up pigs who go back to their own stinking filth and roll around in it.

What is the gospel anyway? It's true freedom! It's the freedom to *not* sin. It's the joy to have a deeper pleasure and infinitely more satisfying pleasure than carnality. The true gospel bids us to say with Paul that everything outside of Christ, as wonderful and pleasurable as it may be, is dung compared to knowing Christ (Phil 3:8). Let us never be the vomit eating dogs or the pigs bathing in filth. Let's live our lives on higher ground, in the power of holiness, the love of Christ, the joy of the Holy Spirit.

Conclusion

Don't be fooled by counterfeit teachers. Those who lift up the name of Christ will live holy lives. Anyone who defends carnal living is a false teacher. Let me appeal to you to take hold of the word of God, and don't let go.

> *Proverbs 4:13* | Keep hold of instruction; do not let go; guard her, for she is your life.

For 13 members of the Hardy family (including children and grandchildren) in Alabama's rural, isolated Calhoun County, there was no time to come up with a survival plan as the sky turned a bizarre shade of green and a tornado formed across a field behind the three mobile homes on the wooded property.

As they watched their homes get ripped apart, 51-year-old Tammy Hardy stumbled into the darkness of the midday with her children and grandchildren into a hollow where they huddled around a clump of three small trees, holding onto each other and the trees as much larger, decades-old trees were ripped out of the ground and tumbled all around them.

They were so desperate that they used a rope to tie the smallest children, Tammy's grandchildren 6-year-old Ben and 5-year-old Nicole, together to keep them from being blown away or running away in fright. They tied a rope around their grandkids and huddled around them in the trees as the storm passed. The father said, "I didn't really have time to think of anything else. I just put it all in God's hands." A family member said that while they had been scratched by flying dirt and debris, none suffered any serious injuries.[113]

Although there are no warning sirens or news alerts, each of us is living in the path of a much more eternal destructive storm. There are false teachers and destructive philosophies abounding around us, and if we do not have a secure place of protection, we will be destroyed.

When the storms of life come, Satan will try to rip you away from Christ, but the only way to stay secure is through our rope, our anchor,

---

[113] The Associated Press, "Small Trees, Rope Save Alabama Family from Tornado." Valdosta Daily Times, September 11, 2014. https://www.valdostadailytimes.com/news/national_and_international/small-trees-rope-save-alabama-family-from-tornado/article_81173a90-9332-5086-8dc0-b5db7025b9f6.html.

the word of God. Don't listen to the false teachers. Huddle with God's remnant people around his word. It's our sure foundation in the storm!

7 | 2 PETER 3:1-7
THE LAST DAYS

By the same word the heavens and earth that now exist are stored up for fire, being kept until the day of judgment and destruction of the ungodly.

2 PETER 3:7

As the menacing clouds of confusion and rebellion envelope our culture, we as believers have a sure hope. We desire to live "a peaceable and quiet life" (1 Tim 2:2) as we await his soon return, but it seems that the trials and troubles of life are so distracting. Peter tells us that we are living in the "last days" of planet earth as we know it. The new creation is on the horizon. Things are getting worse and worse, so how do we live life with the love, joy, and peace of the Spirit in such distracting and confusing times? We must live by the book. Peter tells us that the key to living a contented life in our confusing world is to live by the promises of God's infallible word.

When a plane is suffering a serious emergency, the pilot activates the radio and communicates "mayday" three times. Such a day arrived for Air Sweden, Flight 294 crashed January 8, 2016, but it was entirely preventable. The plane had been flying along just as it should and all appeared normal when suddenly it began to experience all kinds of strange problems. It gyrated across the sky, plummeting thousands of feet at a time and turning violently to one side. One and then two of the four engines stalled and failed, leaving the plane without the power it needed to maintain level flight. The pilot and copilot responded instinctually, doing their best to right the course of the aircraft. Meanwhile hundreds of passengers sat, strapped in their seats, in abject terror, not knowing if they would live or die. The pilots fought valiantly but to no avail.

In the aftermath, investigators found that almost everything that had occurred had been the fault of the pilots. When the plane encountered some turbulence the plane's flight manual told the pilots how to react. But they relied on instinct rather than the book. And then, when the plane began to experience further complications, they ignored the instruments that should have directed them to the source and solution of their problem. They swung the plane violently from side to side attempting to right it because they ignored the aircraft's instrument that told them where the horizon was and how to keep the plane level. They ignored the instruments that told them that their engine problem was not as serious as they thought. Blinded by the stress of the situation, they ignored the manual and did things their own way. Thankfully, no one perished in the flight, but it was pilot error, not relying on the instruments, that caused the disaster in the first place.

Peter speaks of the "last days" (3:3) and says they will be days that are difficult with scoffers tempting the saints to doubt the promise of Christ's return. When Peter speaks of the "last days" he is referring to the time between the first and second comings of Christ. How do we stay strong in these trying times? We need to listen to the vital advice the apostle Peter gives or we will be tossed around and disillusioned in these last days before Christ returns.

STUDY THE WORD (3:1-2)

Peter tells us right away to "stir up" our "sincere minds" with reminders from the word of God.

2 Peter 3:1b | I am stirring up your sincere mind by way of reminder.

We are to constantly contemplate the word. Peter is trying to keep us from being swallowed up by the thinking of this age. We have to look at our instruments or we will most certainly crash. Look to the word of God. Whatever you see with your eyes or feel with your emotions can be deceitful, so don't trust your instincts. Trust God's word. Remember what he said in the first chapter?

> *2 Peter 1:13-15* | I think it right, as long as I am in this body, to stir you up by way of reminder, ¹⁴ since I know that the putting off of my body will be soon, as our Lord Jesus Christ made clear to me. ¹⁵ And I will make every effort so that after my departure you may be able at any time to recall these things.

Peter wrote this letter during his imprisonment in Rome, in the Mamertine prison. He speaks of "my departure" (1:15), and he's referring to his death under the hand of Nero. We know that Peter in 64 A.D. was imprisoned with Paul. Peter was first led away to die. He was told that he would be crucified, but he said that he was not worthy to be crucified in the manner of his Lord Jesus Christ, so he requested to be crucified upside down.[114]

Peter knows he is dying soon, and he wants to stir up their remembrance of the word of God. He implies three things to remember: God's love, God's promises, and God's commands.

God's Word Satisfies

Peter writes his letter to the saints scattered in today's northern Turkey, in order to stir them up and help them remember. We are so prone to forget. He calls them "beloved." How vital it is to remember God's love.

> **2 Peter 3:1a** | This is now the second letter that I am writing to you, beloved.

It is right that many call God's word "a love letter" written to his children. Finding "beloved" in the opening verse of chapter 3 brings a measure of comfort. At long last Peter has come back to the "beloved." Gone, for the moment at least, are the belligerent preachers of the last chapter.[115] As Peter's dying concern, the apostle felt compelled to remind his readers of important truths. Are you experiencing and contemplating the love of God for you on a daily basis?

> *Jeremiah 31:3* | I have loved you, my people, with an everlasting love. With unfailing love I have drawn you to myself.

The Puritan Richard Baxter stated this truth well.

---

[114] Eusebius, *The Ecclesiastical History* (313 A.D.), 3.1; Jerome, *De Viris Illustribus (On Illustrious Men)*, 1.

[115] Helm, *1 & 2 Peter and Jude*, 243.

Is it a small thing in your eyes to be loved by God – to be the son, the spouse, the love, the delight of the King of glory? Christian, believe this, and think about it: you will be eternally embraced in the arms of the love which was from everlasting, and will extend to everlasting – of the love which brought the Son of God's love from heaven to earth, from earth to the cross, from the cross to the grave, from the grave to glory – that love which was weary, hungry, tempted, scorned, scourged, buffeted, spat upon, crucified, pierced – which fasted, prayed, taught, healed, wept, sweated, bled, died. That love will eternally embrace you.[116]

The great God not only loves his saints, but he loves to love them.[117]

God's Word Trasforms

In both Peter's letters, he is reminding us that transformation comes through the mind and heart. We must change from the inside out. We must sincerely stir up our minds with the promises of God's word.

> **2 Peter 3:1b** | In both of them I am stirring up your sincere mind by way of reminder.

We need to listen to God instead of self. I remind you again of the words of Martin Lloyd-Jones the London preacher of a generation ago.

> Have you realized that most of your unhappiness in life is due to the fact that you are listening to yourself instead of talking to yourself?
>
> — *Martyn Lloyd-Jones*

We are called to remind ourselves of God's way of thinking, feeling, and living. We are not called to bitterness, or anxiety, or despair, or foolishness. We are called to love, joy, peace, patience, and wisdom. Remember what Paul says about mind renewal.

> *Ephesians 4:22-24* | To put off your old self, which belongs to your former manner of life and is corrupt through deceitful desires, [23] and to be renewed in the spirit of your minds, [24] and to put on the new self, created after the likeness of God in true righteousness and holiness.

---

[116] Richard Baxter, *The Saints Everlasting Rest* (Leeds, England: Davies and Booth Publishing, 1814), 27.

[117] Jerry Bridges, *Trusting God: Even When Life Hurts* (Colorado Springs, CO: Nav Press, 1988), 142.

David testifies as well.

Psalm 1:2-3 | Blessed is the man who walks not in the counsel of the wicked, nor stands in the way of sinners, nor sits in the seat of scoffers; ² but his delight is in the law of the Lord, and on his law he meditates day and night. ³ He is like a tree planted by streams of water that yields its fruit in its season, and its leaf does not wither. In all that he does, he prospers.

What are some ways we can stir up a sincere and pure mind by mind renewal? Here are a few that come to mind: daily read and study Scripture, discuss Scripture with other believers, pray through Scripture, counsel yourself, including your emotions, with Scripture, act quickly in obedience to Scripture, plan ahead what you will do in temptation according to Scripture, talk to yourself instead of listening to yourself, fight lies with truth from Scripture.

If you are not continually connected to Scripture, counseling yourself with Scripture, you will lose the sense of God's presence. God's love is the most real thing in the universe. If you don't sense it, it means you are allowing your heart to be hardened. Let Scripture wake you up to his love. Renew your mind with God's peace. Truly, we say with Isaiah, "You will keep him in perfect peace, whose mind is stayed on you, because he trusts in you" (Isa 26:3).

God's Word Motivates

2 Peter 3:2a | That you should remember the predictions of the holy prophets.

If you are not aware of Bible prophecy, you are going to crash in this life. Theologians would say our eschatology should inform our soteriology. In other words, what happens in the end of the world should affect your life right now. Peter tells us to remember the prophecies of the Old Testament. Which ones did Peter have in mind? He's referring to the end of history, that final day of judgment and salvation.[118] We are not just following Christ in order to "live our best life now." We are living for another world, the new creation. The consummation of all things is at hand saints. Don't covet this world's goods because it's all going to burn up!

---

[118] Schreiner, *1, 2 Peter, Jude*, 370.

This world will most certainly come to an end. It won't be the result of the exhaustion of physical resources. Many nonbelieving scientists also hold that the world will come to an end—for instance, when the physical properties that fuel the sun are completely used up. In one sense, then, a simple belief that the world will end is nothing special. It is shared by Christians and non-Christians alike. What is unique to the apostolic gospel is that the end will come by the intentional command and word of God—in the very hour he so decides—to give final supremacy to his Son and draw the curtain down in judgment on that which he began.[119] The weary, worn out, sin-cursed earth will be burnt down and remade. A new creation of everlasting joy will give way to the sad and miserable state of our present world. Keep that in mind when you see the instability of this life.

Let me repeat that Peter's primary source of what happens at the end of time with the second coming of Christ is found in the prophecies of the Hebrew Scriptures. Throughout the Old Testament, the prophets continually predict God's final eschatological judgment. For example, Isaiah proclaims:

> *Isaiah 66:15-16* | For behold, the Lord will come in fire and his chariots like the whirlwind, to render his anger with fury, and his rebuke with flames of fire. For the Lord will execute judgment by fire and by his sword on all flesh, and those slain by the Lord will be many (*cf* Isa 13:10–13; 24:19–23; 34:1–4; 51:6).

Similarly, Malachi tells us that the lost and arrogant, and all who live outside of God's guidance should be frightened about what's about to happen.

> *Malachi 4:1-2* | For behold, the day is coming, burning like an oven, when all the arrogant and all evildoers will be stubble. The day that is coming shall set them ablaze, says the Lord of hosts, so that it will leave them neither root nor branch. ² But for you who fear my name, the sun of righteousness shall rise with healing in its wings.

Malachi says: be looking to Christ who is like a winged sun that will guide you and bring you light and life and healing. Also, as New Testament saints, we also have the incredible privilege of hearing exactly what the apostles looked for concerning the end of the world.

---

[119] Helm, *1 & 2 Peter and Jude*, 246.

2 Peter 3:10-13 | The day of the Lord will come like a thief, and then the heavens will pass away with a roar, and the heavenly bodies will be burned up and dissolved, and the earth and the works that are done on it will be exposed. [11] Since all these things are thus to be dissolved, what sort of people ought you to be in lives of holiness and godliness, [12] waiting for and hastening the coming of the day of God, because of which the heavens will be set on fire and dissolved, and the heavenly bodies will melt as they burn! [13] But according to his promise we are waiting for new heavens and a new earth in which righteousness dwells.

How should our lives and attitudes be as we await his coming? We should always be thinking about the sudden, sovereign coming of the Lord (*cf* Mt 24:30-31). Thinking about the end helps us lower the value of anything earthly and live with a kingdom mindset (*cf* Phil 3:8; Mt 6:33). As you read God's word, it's preparing you for the world to come, and that's quite the motivation!

God's Word Demands

Now Peter reminds us that living this kind of life where we apply God's word continually to our lives is not optional. It's a command!

2 Peter 3:2a | And the commandment of the Lord and Savior through your apostles.

I really like this—we often say that you should apply the word of God to your life and live it out. When I say *should*, I could be misleading you. It's not an option. We *must* do it. God demands it.

Peter emphasizes that the commands of the apostles' writings actually represented the words of Jesus Christ as Lord and Savior.[120] What Peter is saying is that all the words that the apostles write in the New Testament are from what Jesus has taught. They are not just to be understood in theory but applied and obeyed in our lives. God demands it!

God's word is not just a suggestion, but a command. God designed life to be lived in a certain way. That's why sin brings misery. The entire New Testament is not just to be contemplated but obeyed. This is Peter's point. Remember the words of James.

---

[120] Schreiner, *1, 2 Peter, Jude.*, 371.

James 1:22-25 | But be doers of the word, and not hearers only, deceiving yourselves. [23] For if anyone is a hearer of the word and not a doer, he is like a man who looks intently at his natural face in a mirror. [24] For he looks at himself and goes away and at once forgets what he was like. [25] But the one who looks into the perfect law, the law of liberty, and perseveres, being no hearer who forgets but a doer who acts, he will be blessed in his doing.

Examine your own life as Peter said. We are to apply the word of God on a daily basis. Peter told us in no uncertain terms to do just that in chapter 1.

2 Peter 1:10 | Be all the more diligent to confirm your calling and election, for if you practice these qualities you will never fall.

Moses tells us the same thing in Deuteronomy 6. After he reviews the ten commandments in the fifth chapter, the Lord summarizes his commands and tells us how to obey them. We are to live them out in every area of life.

Deuteronomy 6:4-9 | Hear, O Israel: The Lord our God, the Lord is one. [5] You shall love the Lord your God with all your heart and with all your soul and with all your might. [6] And these words that I command you today shall be on your heart. [7] You shall teach them diligently to your children, and shall talk of them when you sit in your house, and when you walk by the way, and when you lie down, and when you rise. [8] You shall bind them as a sign on your hand, and they shall be as frontlets between your eyes. [9] You shall write them on the doorposts of your house and on your gates.

In every aspect of life, we are to learn to consider God's demands on us. We are his children, his creation. He designed how to live life and we disobey it to our peril and misery. Be sure you are not just an information gatherer but an obedient follower of the Lord.

SHUN THE WORLD (3:3-6)

One of the things that gets us off course is the world's attack against the way of life Christ designed for us to live. We get a bit dizzy with all the trials, discouragements, and tribulations we face each day. We must never get our hope and joy and purpose from the world. In fact, Peter tells us to shun all the doubters and scoffers in the world.

What are some ways that the world scoffs at Christianity? We see it in morality with their promiscuity, immorality, and gender blending.

We see it in science with their far-fetched idea of evolution informing their understanding for how the world began. We are going to see that people are much more willing to believe myths than to trust the living God.

We have to be careful not to be taken into the world's thinking. We are called to live a life separate from the world. Remember John's warning.

> *1 John 2:15-17* | Do not love the world or the things in the world. If anyone loves the world, the love of the Father is not in him. ⁶ For all that is in the world—the desires of the flesh and the desires of the eyes and pride of life—is not from the Father but is from the world. ¹⁷ And the world is passing away along with its desires, but whoever does the will of God abides forever.

What are some ways that we are easily drawn away by the world? Often, we think of movies and media, but our emotions are just as prone to draw us away from Christ. Every temptation and lie of Satan can be defeated if we "put on the whole armor of God" which is a metaphor for trusting God, putting on the word and walking in the Spirit. We've got to live a life that is not influenced by the scoffers around us (*cf* Psa 1:1-2).

The Danger of Scoffers

2 Peter 3:3a | Knowing this first of all, that scoffers will come in the last days with scoffing.

The time they appear. The appearance of scoffers should not be a surprise to us. They will try to infiltrate the church in the "last days." Peter now introduces the timing and paradigm of this age of grace, which he calls the "last days." The "last days" is a way of describing the time on earth between the first and second comings of Christ. The idea is that the Christian having citizenship on earth, should live life through his or her citizenship in heaven. Your body is on earth, in Ephesus, or Chicago, or wherever you live, but your spirit is with Christ "seated in the heavenly realm" (Eph 2:6). Our hearts are in heaven, but Peter says that scoffers, those who reject God and his word, are all around us on earth in these last days. We should not be surprised by scoffers, but know they will be among us, always attacking, mocking, and tearing down the glory of the gospel in very sophisticated way.

The activity they promote. Peter says that scoffers will come "with scoffing." It's what they are good at. Peter was getting ready to pass off the scene, and he wanted the believers to be able to protect themselves from the dangerous influence of scoffers when he was gone. Scoffers can dull and harden our hearts by exposing and influencing Christians to sinful and selfish ways of living. We've seen the tempo and volume of mockery intensify in America. On TV, in the media, in movies, over the airwaves, and on the Internet, the scoffers have become bolder as American culture in general has become more pagan. Atheism, humanism, materialism, and a hedonistic paganism have become the norm among the world today, and it doesn't seem to be changing.[121] Slowly, the world will cool the fire of Christians and "because lawlessness will be increased, the love of many will grow cold" (Mt 24:12).

Not only that, but scoffers are so influential in twenty-first century America, that cancel-culture is becoming a way of "ex-communication" in their cult of secularism and humanism. Scoffers don't want the light of Christians to expose them.

The danger they present. It's hard to avoid scoffers since are everywhere. They are dangerous, so they are to be avoided at all costs. They may even try to deceive you "having a form of godliness but denying its power." Turn away from them.

> *2 Timothy 3:1-5* | But know this, that in the last days perilous times will come: ² For men will be lovers of themselves, lovers of money, boasters, proud, blasphemers, disobedient to parents, unthankful, unholy, ³ unloving, unforgiving, slanderers, without self-control, brutal, despisers of good, ⁴ traitors, headstrong, haughty, lovers of pleasure rather than lovers of God, ⁵ having a form of godliness but denying its power. And from such people turn away!

The influence of scoffers permeates the airwaves and media of our time. The propaganda of the evolution has been disproven even by secular scientists, and yet it is used as an almost religious litmus test to keep scientists toeing the party line. Why is believing in evolution so vital for the secular worldview? Because a biblical worldview involves accountability for all our actions. If God is at the center of all that we see and experience, then we must truly stand before him on the last day.

---

[121] Swindoll, *Insights on James and 1 & 2 Peter*, 314.

It is vital part of the enemy's plan for the media to mock Christians and to paint them as backwards and ignorant. For so-called progressives, evolution is "the touchstone that separates the enlightened from the ignorant."[122] This couldn't be farther from the truth. Darwinian evolution is bogus science. They have no scientific proof. There's nothing in geology (fossils in the rocks) and nothing in biology that demonstrates hybrid. Irreducible complexity in biology has ruled out the possibility of evolution. We have no record. All we have is gaps of incredible amounts of time. And we are supposed to believe that with vast amounts of time, yet no evidence, that all things evolved from a primordial soup where life magically began. No evidence, just billions of years.

So what is the best they can do? Famed evolutionary biologist and noted atheist Richard Dawkins has floated a fanciful idea, suggesting that extraterrestrials may be responsible for a possible "signature of intelligence" in life. Indeed, no less a scientific genius than Francis Crick, who helped discover DNA, also proposed the idea that ET's seeded life on earth to set the evolutionary process in motion. So why have these scientists considered this seemingly far-fetched possibility? Because they have encountered a big mystery they can't explain. It turns out that even the simplest living cells aren't simple at all, and that discovery has made it extremely difficult to explain the origin of life.[123] The foundation of evolutionary biology today is... aliens. That's truly laughable.

Yet the media, using popular personalities will openly mock Christians on national television. Actor Matt Damon, for instance, was horrified that a Christian (Sarah Palin), could become Vice President of the United States. Here him mock Christians: "I need to know if she really thinks dinosaurs were here 4,000 years ago. That's important – I want to know that. I really do because she's going to have the nuclear codes."[124] Damon scoffs. He knows what he believes. If we are all simply accidents of nature – of no more worth than animals – then abortion is no more offensive than hunting. Gay marriage is irrelevant. Gender

---

[122] William Dembski in July Roys, *The Evolution Litmus Test*. (Chicago: The Roys Report, December 5, 2014), julieroys.com/the-evolution-litmus-test.

[123] Stephen C. Meyer, *Aliens, the Multiverse, or God?* (Seattle, WA: Discovery Institute, December 22, 2021), discovery.org/v/aliens-multiverse-god.

[124] Rachel Weiner, *Palin Claimed Dinosaurs and People Coexisted*. (New York: HuffPost, May 25, 2011), huffpost.com/entry/palin-claimed-dinosaurs-a_n_130012.

blending is not a dysphoria but now it is a right. But if God is at the center of everything (and he is), then the scoffers are revealed to be those who are cosmically and *deliberately* ignorant (*cf* 3:5).

The Depravity of Scoffers

Whether or not they admit it, immorality is the real reason that scoffers mock and deny the second coming. They love the pleasure of sin for a season. These scoffers are enslaved to their sinful and selfish desires.

2 Peter 3:3b-7 | Following their own sinful desires.

They follow, or literally "travel," after their God-rejecting sinful desires. This denotes a pattern of long-term behavior, faithfully following themselves instead of God. They scoff at God, determined to fashion a god in their own image.[125] They "love darkness rather than light because their deeds are evil" (Jn 3:19).

In contrast, believers embrace the fact that the Lord will return (Acts 1:10–11), that they will give account for their lives (Rom 14:12; 2 Cor 5:10), and that he will bestow rewards based on faithfulness (1 Cor 3:12–15). They also believe that when Christ comes, he will reveal the secret things of the heart (1 Cor 4:5). Those who truly hope in his return have an incentive for holy living (Phil 3:20–21; 4:1; 1 Jn 3:2–3) because they realize that "each one of us will give an account of himself to God" (Rom 14:12).[126]

The Doubts of Scoffers

The same doubt people had for the flood of Noah's day, they have with the consummation.

2 Peter 3:4 | They will say, "Where is the promise of his coming? For ever since the fathers fell asleep, all things are continuing as they were from the beginning of creation."

They scoff at Christ's return because years have passed, and it has not happened— the laws of science continue as they have from the beginning of creation. In modern times, that view is known as uniformitarianism. It is good and true enough that the laws of God continue as

---

[125] Helm, *1 & 2 Peter and Jude*, 244.
[126] MacArthur, *2 Peter and Jude*, 113.

they are. Yet, unbelievers maintain that God's promise is unreliable, and that God's universe is a stable, unchanging system where events like the second coming just do not happen.[127] It categorically denies divine intervention throughout world history, most notably opposing both six-day creation and the global Flood.

To be sure, if the natural laws and universal processes did not normally function in a consistent manner, chaos would ensue. Yet a biblical view of the universe, sees creation as an *open* system—in which God has ordained a uniform operation of natural causes, but also a universe in which he has intervened and still does intervene.[128] Indeed Christ can come at any moment and interrupt the normal stability of creation, and indeed, he will!

The Denial of Scoffers

They can live thinking the earth will go on as it is, because they purposefully deny that the earth was formed miraculously.

> **2 Peter 3:5-7** | For they deliberately overlook this fact, that the heavens existed long ago, and the earth was formed out of water and through water by the word of God, **6** and that by means of these the world that then existed was deluged with water and perished.

The world was formed through supernatural means, it was judged by supernatural means, and one day it will be recreated through supernatural means.

Science will always confirm the Scriptures, I found it fascinating that the story of Genesis can be seen in modern science. I read an article from the New York Times dated March 9, 2008, that seemed to agree with the Biblical account. Kenneth Chang writes that scientists now believe that the universe began as an instantaneous event.

> A cosmic inflation, a rapid expansion of the universe in the first trillionth of a trillionth of a second of its existence.[129]

---

[127] Green, *2 Peter and Jude*, 150.
[128] MacArthur., *Acts*, 114.
[129] Kenneth Chang, *Gauging Age of Universe Becomes More Precise* (New York: New York Times Newspaper, March 9, 2008). Retrieved May 4, 2022, from https://www.nytimes.com/2008/03/09/science/space/09cosmos.html

This discovery corresponds exactly with what the Scriptures have taught us all along: that in the beginning, the Lord stretched out the universe (*cf* Isa 40:22). The universe began by supernatural means. Scientists can't explain how order came from chaos. They theorize that all began when a black hole reversed. They can depersonalize God, but he is not a black hole. He is the infinite Creator of all things. And if you accept that premise, it is not difficult to understand how God will judge the earth. He gave us a dress rehearsal with the worldwide flood.

Peter links the global judgment of the flood with the coming judgment at Christ's coming. If you want to understand how God will judge the world, look to Noah. In the days before the flood, the people mocked. And just as then, they are mocking now. But they will not mock when Jesus returns. Consider the prophecy of Revelation.

> *Revelation 6:12-17* | I looked, and behold, there was a great earthquake, and the sun became black as sackcloth, the full moon became like blood, [13] and the stars of the sky fell to the earth as the fig tree sheds its winter fruit when shaken by a gale. [14] The sky vanished like a scroll that is being rolled up, and every mountain and island was removed from its place. [15] Then the kings of the earth and the great ones and the generals and the rich and the powerful, and everyone, slave and free, hid themselves in the caves and among the rocks of the mountains, [16] calling to the mountains and rocks, "Fall on us and hide us from the face of him who is seated on the throne, and from the wrath of the Lamb, [17] for the great day of their wrath has come, and who can stand?"

ANTICIPATE THE LORD (3:7)

We are called to live in light of the Lord's coming. Have you ever had a moment, where you thought—this is it! Jesus must be coming again! Perhaps it was a dream. Maybe you awoke in the night thinking Christ's return had begun. Many times, I've seen the sun shining so brightly through the clouds, I thought, he could return right now! The truth is, we don't know when Christ will return.

The Consummation is Sudden

> *2 Peter 3:10* | The day of the Lord will come like a thief, and then the heavens will pass away with a roar.

We have to be ready at all times. The second coming take place "in a moment, in the twinkling of an eye" (1 Cor 15:52). That means the second coming of Christ will happen suddenly. It will happen instantaneously. We can't know when exactly it will occur. I can't wait, what about you?

> Matthew 24:30, 36 | They will see the Son of Man coming on the clouds of heaven with power and great glory. ³⁶ "But concerning that day and hour no one knows..."

No one can know the timing of the second coming, but we know it is imminent. That means like the early Christians, we should be looking for Jesus to come at any moment. This is the way the apostles lived and taught. At any moment, Christ could come. Those early Christians 2000 years ago were waiting for Jesus. Our gaze must ever be set to heaven, looking for the return of the one who rose from the dead.

> Titus 2:13 | Looking for the blessed hope and glorious appearing of our great God and Savior Jesus Christ.

Dear saints, what am I saying? I am saying that Jesus may come before you finish this sentence. All Christians have always had this hope.

The Consummation is Sovereign

God alone directs when and how the consummation will occur.

> **2 Peter 3:7a** | But by the same word the heavens and earth that now exist are stored up for fire.

The first judgment was one of water, but at the second coming, the earth will be consumed through fire. God is not going to utterly destroy the earth, but recreate it as a new heaven and earth, where there is no wickedness.

Don't put your trust in anything on earth since you can't take any of it with you. Lay up treasure in heaven. Set your eyes on things above, not on things on the earth (Col 3:1-3).

The Consummation is Shocking

The day is coming, and when the heavens and earth will dissolve with fire, and it will shock the ungodly.

> **2 Peter 3:7b** | Being kept until the day of judgment and destruction of the ungodly.

The lost will be shocked when Jesus comes again, be we as saints are comforted. The heavens and earth are being kept going until the day of judgment, which means "destruction for the ungodly." Imagine as a lost person you have put all your stock in this world. You have ignored God and lived the way you want. Suddenly the sky opens up with a glorious sight. There he is! Jesus! But you've denied him. So what happens?

> *Revelation 6:15-16* | Then the kings of the earth and the great ones and the generals and the rich and the powerful, and everyone, slave and free, hid themselves in the caves and among the rocks of the mountains, ¹⁶ calling to the mountains and rocks, "Fall on us and hide us from the face of him who is seated on the throne, and from the wrath of the Lamb, ¹⁷ for the great day of their wrath has come, and who can stand?"

Without Christ, the lost world has no hope. They hope the mountains and the rocks will fall on them to save them from the wrath of the Lamb. Without the gospel, this lost world has no hope. Let's not be sleeping saints. We need to let our light shine before men. Give the gospel. "How shall they hear without a preacher?" Who will tell them if you don't? And we must not participate in the unfruitful works of darkness. Have nothing to do with the ungodly's way of life. Be ready, for Christ's return is completely unexpected for the lost, like a thief in the night. We believers on the other hand are not sleeping but awake, waiting and expecting the surprise.

> *1 Thessalonians 5:2-6* | You yourselves are fully aware that the day of the Lord will come like a thief in the night. ³ While people are saying, "There is peace and security," then sudden destruction will come upon them as labor pains come upon a pregnant woman, and they will not escape. ⁴ But you are not in darkness, brothers, for that day to surprise you like a thief. ⁵ For you are all children of light, children of the day. We are not of the night or of the darkness. ⁶ So then let us not sleep, as others do, but let us keep awake and be sober.

Dear saints, we must not allow the propaganda of the news media to guide our lives. Nor should we follow our emotions or the unstable circumstances of this world. Rather, we need to keep our eyes on the instrument panel God gave us: his inspired, infallible, everlasting, forever settled in heaven, word of God!

Conclusion

A mother was explaining to her little girl, the death of her father. The mother said: "God has sent for your father and will send for us, but I do not know just when."

Finally, the little girl said: "If we do not know just when God is going to send for us, do you not think we had better pack up and get ready to go? God might send when we are not ready."

Let's always remain ready for Christ's coming and live godly lives as we point people to a kingdom that will never fade away.

8 | 2 PETER 3:8-13

THE SECOND COMING

God's word
2 PETER 1:15-16

Have you ever had a dream about the second coming of Christ? That's happened several times where I dream about the clouds opening and seeing the glory and power of Jesus. Suddenly I'm awake thinking at any second, I'm going to be with the Lord in the air, only to realize it's a dream.

One day, it won't be a dream. Jesus will return. Can you imagine? Saints, when he returns our true life will begin. Your sin will be remembered no more. Most people on the earth live for this life only. They are not planning for eternity. They are so nearsighted that they just want to make it through the day. They put off thinking about the Lord's second coming.

THE SURETY OF CHRIST'S COMING (3:8-9)

People let their money and pleasure blind their eyes, numbing themselves with entertainment. They even try and deny his coming. But for the saints, we long for the second coming of Jesus. It's at the center of all we do.

Because the Lord is Transcendent

The Lord is coming, we can be sure of that. Sometimes it seems like such a long time, but we must remember that the timing is based on God's plan and prerogative, not ours. God is infinitely bigger than us!

One of the things that gives every Christian peace, if we choose to focus on it, is the Lord's transcendence. That means God is so big, he transcends our problems. He transcends the universe and exists outside of time and space. If it seems like the Lord is delaying his coming, it's because time for God is nothing.

> **2 Peter 3:8** | But do not overlook this one fact, beloved, that with the Lord one day is as a thousand years, and a thousand years as one day.

Peter quotes the Psalm of Moses—Psalm 90—and helps us to understand why it might be taking so long for the Lord to return.

> *Psalm 90:4* | For a thousand years in your sight are like yesterday when it passes by, or as a watch in the night.

Because God is so big, a moment is no different from an eon, and millenniums pass like moments to the eternal God. What may seem like a long time to believers, like a thousand years, is actually quite short, like one day, in God's sight. While Christ's return may seem afar off to us, it is imminent from God's perspective.[130] At any moment Christ may return.

Often in teaching about the last days, we get concerned about how the timing and events line up for Christ's return. What you need to know is that all the events have been in motion since the resurrection of Christ. He could have returned in the apostles' lifetime. Christ told us in Matthew 24 that all the signs of the time were set in motion already. We've been seeing these signs since the life of the apostles. Jesus speaks of many signs of his coming (Mt 24:4-22) including: false teachers, wars and rumors of wars, persecution, famines, earthquakes, a falling away, increased lawlessness in the laws of society, discouraged but enduring Christians, gospel preaching, among many other things.

Dear saints, God transcends us. He is exalted above the heavens (Psa 8:1; 57:5). He is enthroned on high (Psa 113:5) as the most high (Psa 97:9). No one is above him. He is separate from his creation and

---

[130] MacArthur, *2 Peter and Jude*, 121.

not dependent upon his creation in any way. We make a great mistake trying to measure time from our own puny, finite, human perspective. It is much better to surrender by faith to God's timing since he is the sovereign one.

Because the Lord is Tenderhearted

Tender in patience. God's heart matches the bigness of his person. He's patient toward sinners. The reason he's delaying the coming of Christ is not because he's forgotten his promise to renew all things, but he's calling sinners from everywhere to come to into the kingdom.

> **2 Peter 3:9** | The Lord is not slow to fulfill his promise as some count slowness, but is patient toward you, not wishing that any should perish, but that all should reach repentance.

Tender in love. God knows and loves your loved ones more than you. If you have a burden for the lost, it came from God first. He "loved the world" in such an infinite way that he gave his own Son, the one and only Messiah (Jn 3:16). He's waiting because his love makes him patient.

Tender in mercy. God is "not wishing that any should perish." God is not indifferent toward the lost. He delays so that sinners would repent. Repentance means a "change of mind and perspective." It's a one-eighty turn to hate what you once loved and love what you once.

Tender to all. God wants "all" to "reach repentance." How do we reconcile this with the doctrine of election and predestination? I don't know, and I don't need to know. Spurgeon said the doctrine of God's sovereignty in salvation and man's responsibility in salvation are like two train tracks cannot be reconciled on earth but only when we reach the throne of God. On the outside of the gates of heaven, it says, "Whosoever will may come." One the inside, it says, "Elect from the foundation of the world." How God wants all to reach repentance. He has "no pleasure in the death of the wicked" (Eze 18:23). Spurgeon said it this way:

> If sinners be damned, at least let them leap to hell over our dead bodies. And if they perish, let them perish with our arms wrapped about their knees, imploring them to stay. If hell must be filled, let it be filled

in the teeth of our exertions, and let not one go unwarned and un-prayed for.[131]

Let us be tender to the lost, not willing that any should perish, with a heart like our compassionate God. Let us never give up hope for any of our friends, family, loved ones, strangers, and even our enemies.

THE SHOCK OF CHRIST'S COMING

There are many signs that precede the coming of Christ, which have been since the time of Christ's first coming. We've seen epidemics, wars and rumors of wars, natural disasters, and lawlessness increasing in our laws and society (i.e., homosexual marriage). The signs of Christ's coming are already here and have been increasing since the first coming of Christ. Each generation prepares for the second coming of Christ.

The Suddenness of the End

Jesus said, "concerning that day and hour no one knows" (Mt 24:36). Yet people try to predict it. No one will be watching except Christians. For the lost, Jesus coming will be like an unexpected intruder.

> **2 Peter 3:10a** | But the day of the Lord will come like a thief.

I want to emphasize that though Christians don't know the day or the hour, we are prepared at all times for the coming of Jesus. It's the centerpiece of our lives. It's what we live for. We keep our lamps full of oil and burning brightly with extra flasks of oil (Mt 25:1-13). Be prepared because the end comes suddenly. Listen to Jesus in Mark 13.

> *Mark 13:32-33* | But concerning that day or that hour, no one knows, not even the angels in heaven, nor the Son, but only the Father. ³³ Be on guard, keep awake. For you do not know when the time will come.

Paul gives us the application of Jesus words in his letter to the Thessalonians.

> *1 Thessalonians 5:2-6* | You yourselves are fully aware that the day of the Lord will come like a thief in the night. ³ While people are saying, "There is peace and security," then sudden destruction will come upon them as labor pains come upon a pregnant woman, and they will

---

[131] Charles Spurgeon, "The Wailing of Risca" in *Metropolitan Tabernacle Pulpit*, Vol 7 (London: Passmore and Alabaster, 1861), 9.

not escape. ⁴ But you are not in darkness, brothers, for that day to surprise you like a thief. ⁵ For you are all children of light, children of the day. We are not of the night or of the darkness. ⁶ So then let us not sleep, as others do, but let us keep awake and be sober.

Stay sober! Don't numb yourself with media, substance, or immoral behavior. Stay far away from the temptation to find your joy and peace in the world. There is only pleasure in sin for a season. Instead, be filled with the joy of the Holy Spirit, looking forward to the moment when Jesus splits the clouds in glory and power, bringing with him the rest of the new creation!

The Severity of the End

If you think you can make it through the second coming, you are seriously mistaken. The severity of Jesus' return is so fierce that the cosmos will melt. Planets and stars, the moon and the sun will be dissolved by the glory of our Lord's return.

> **2 Peter 3:10b** | And then the heavens will pass away with a roar, and the heavenly bodies will be burned up and dissolved, and the earth and the works that are done on it will be exposed.

Despite the delay, the day of the Lord *will* come. It will mark the end of God's forbearance, and so it threatens the unrepentant, the proud, and the worldly. And Peter goes on to describe it in descriptive apocalyptic language from the Old Testament and the words of Jesus. Jesus had spoken of 'signs in the sun, moon, and stars. On the earth, nations will be in anguish and perplexity' (Lk 21:25). Peter turned to his Old Testament for further illumination. Passages such in Isaiah (13:10–13; 24:19; 64:1–4; 66:16) and Micah (1:4) would have come to mind, especially Isaiah 34.[132]

> *Isaiah 34:4* | All the stars of the heavens will be dissolved and the sky rolled up like a scroll.

With the rumbling of thunder, and the crackle of flames, the sky will be dissolved, rolling up like a scroll. The earth will be aflame. All the earthly treasures that people invested in will burn up. All the beautiful cars and houses and boats will perish. All the luxurious vacation spots will vanish. All banks, all money, all treasures will be gone

---

[132] Green, *2 Peter and Jude*, 161.

forever. The world will be shaken, and that which cannot be shaken—our faith—will remain.

THE SANCTITY OF CHRIST'S COMING

As we consider that earthly things are eternally worthless, it should affect how we see the present state of the world.

Our Faithfulness

God's people we see what the lost cannot see. We are loyal to the King of kings. Unbelievers are blinded to the beauty of eternal things. They have no problem doing unseemly things and numbing themselves to the pain of this world through any means possible. Only believers in Christ can truly appreciate the temporal nature of things and live a sanctified life.

> **2 Peter 3:11** | Since all these things are thus to be dissolved, what sort of people ought you to be in lives of holiness and godliness.

Since everything we see with our eyes is going to perish, we ought not hope in the things of this world. Instead of loving money and pleasure, we ought to have pleasure in expanding Christ's kingdom, first and foremost, by living lives that are in conformity to Christ. Peter covered this in chapter 1. If we do not choose to live in holiness, Peter has already warned us that a Christian can become "so nearsighted that he is blind, having forgotten that he was cleansed from his former sins. Therefore, brothers, be all the more diligent to confirm your calling and election" (1:9-10).

Our Focus

As believers we understand the futility of the earth. We groan with all creation for the new creation to arrive. We wait and hasten Christ's coming.

> **2 Peter 3:12** | Waiting for and hastening the coming of the day of God, because of which the heavens will be set on fire and dissolved, and the heavenly bodies will melt as they burn!

Our focus is quite different than the lost. Our focus then negatively is that we must live lives separate from the ways of the world (1 Jn 3:15-16). The lust of the eyes and the lust of the flesh and the pride of life should never characterize the saints of God. Positively, we should have our focus should be on "things above."

> *Colossians 3:1-4* | If then you have been raised with Christ, seek the things that are above, where Christ is, seated at the right hand of God. ² Set your minds on things that are above, not on things that are on earth. ³ For you have died, and your life is hidden with Christ in God. ⁴ When Christ who is your life appears, then you also will appear with him in glory.

Why should we, the saints of God, be interested in any of the worthless things on earth? The truth is, we cannot even begin to joy life the way God designed it until we are surrendered to him. We enjoy family because Christ is at the center. We enjoy food and the pleasures of life because Christ is the center of all we do. "Whether we eat or drink or whatsoever you do," Paul says, "do all to the glory of God" (1 Cor 10:31). Life actually cannot be enjoyed without our hearts completely surrendered to Jesus.

We also do the work of evangelism and share the gospel, and as we do, we participate in speeding the return of Christ. God already knows how many and who will be saved, and when that number is fulfilled, the end will come (Mt 24:14; Rom 11:24–25). Don't go overboard on this, though. There's no way for us to know who or how many, so even though it's true that our work of evangelism hastens the end, we may be doing our work in the middle of his timetable![133]

Our Future

"This world is not our home! We're just a passin' through. My treasures are laid up somewhere beyond the blue!" Our future is not in the ways of this world. Our life is just "a vapor that appears for a little while and then vanishes away." What fools we would be to lay up our treasure on earth.

> **2 Peter 3:12** | But according to his promise we are waiting for new heavens and a new earth in which righteousness dwells.

When many Christians think about eternal life, often the thought is only of "heaven." Here Peter envisions not only a new heaven but also

---

[133] Swindoll, *Insights on James and 1 & 2 Peter*, 323.

a new earth, presumably the dwelling place of God's people.[134] The glory and joy of this prophesy comes directly from the prophet Isaiah.

> *Isaiah 65:17-18* | For behold, I create new heavens and a new earth, and the former things shall not be remembered or come into mind. [18] But be glad and rejoice forever in that which I create; for behold, I create Jerusalem to be a joy, and her people to be a gladness.

The same fire that strikes terror into the heart of the mockers brings hope to the believer since it means the end of the sin cursed earth has finally come. There in the new heaven and earth we will enjoy the new creation and worship God without distraction. Sin, which has marred God's world, will not be permitted to have the final word. In a renewed universe the ravages of the fall will be repaired by the glory of the restoration. Paradise Lost will become Paradise Regained, and God's will shall eventually be done alike in earth and heaven.[135] There's coming a day when we shall walk through the pearly gates and walk on the streets of gold. We will have a resurrection body that has no capability for sin. All evil will have been destroyed. The nations of the saved will have no desire but to do their heavenly Father's will. The wicked will be destroyed, and the righteous will shine like the sun in the kingdom of their Father (Mt 13:41–43).[136] There will be no more misery or pain. You will never feel anxiety or anger ever again. The former things will forever pass away.

Conclusion

I've dreamed about the second coming of Jesus, and it seems so real, but one day Jesus will actually come. In the meantime, we are called to be conformed to his image.

Sometimes in tornado season in the Midwest we will have a warning that says, "This is a test of the Emergency Broadcast System." It warns us of tornadoes and other dangerous weather. Once as a child on the southside of Chicago where we lived at 147th and Central, I looked up from our back porch and to my shock there were funnel clouds. We had heard warning all day, but I was so curious about the green sky and the beautiful funnels coming down. My dad was at work, and mom was shouting for us to get down to the basement. I had never seen those

---

[134] Black, *1 & 2 Peter*, 2 Pe 3:13.
[135] Green, *2 Peter and Jude*, 165.
[136] Ibid., 166.

funnel clouds before, but I'll never forget the day when the test became real.

We see the signs of the times. They are telling us that something and truly someone is coming, and we need to be ready. We've waited and waited, but one day the moment will be real. Jesus will return. And all will be well!

9 | 2 PETER 3:14-18
GROW IN GRACE

But grow in the grace and knowledge of our Lord and Savior Jesus Christ. To him be the glory both now and to the day of eternity. Amen.

2 PETER 3:18

We end with Peter where he began: grow in grace! Jesus is coming, so we need to progress in discipleship with our Lord. When I was a child, my parents wanted me to grow up normally. There was just one problem: I had a serious heart murmur, a VSD: ventricular septal defect. Essentially, because of a hole between my left and right lower ventricles, my heart would back up with blood. The valve in one of my heart's chambers had a hole in it, and it wouldn't close completely. So the surgeon had to go in and do major open heart surgery. I was just three years old, but I remember as if it was yesterday. That kind of surgery upended my entire family's life. My dad and others took care of the five other children. And my mom stayed with me in the hospital. The result is that I will live a lot longer and have a better quality of life. Instead of dying young of heart failure, I'll be able to live a lot longer. I just turned forty-eight this year, so it must've worked.

If it's important to make hard decisions to grow physically, how much more important is it to do the hard things that will help us grow spiritually, since that is the purpose of our lives.

PROGRESS IN YOUR WALK (3:14)

No disrespect to Peter, but he is the most loudmouthed and plain of all the apostles. He even complains a bit (under inspiration of the Spirit) that Paul's letters are "hard to read" at times. You don't have to guess with Peter. He tells us plainly four ways that we can progress in our walk with Christ.

Through Patience

The first thing he says we need in order to grow is a spirit of patience as we await Christ's coming.

> **2 Peter 3:14** | Therefore, beloved, since you are waiting for these, be diligent to be found by him without spot or blemish, and at peace.

Peter tells us to be "waiting" for these things to come to pass. That's what this life is: a lot of waiting. We are not to be waiting and hoping for our next raise or our next car. Sure, we will do that, but it ought not consume us or be the center of our hope. We have hopes and dreams for our family, for our calling and vocation, for our legacy. But those things are always subordinate to what we are really waiting for. Where should our hope be?

> *Matthew 6:33* | Seek first the kingdom of God and his righteousness, and all these things shall be added unto you.

When I was 16, I met the girl who is now my wife. She ended up going a different direction and went to nursing school in another state. But she loved Jesus. She was beautiful and godly—the girl of my dreams. I wouldn't settle for any other girl. With her father's permission, I pursued her. I wrote her. I called her. I put her first. I waited for her. She's a year younger, so I moved to Chicago, got a good paying job, and asked her to marry me. I waited. I pursued. But finally, the wedding day arrived. It was worth the wait!

It wasn't easy waiting. There were many temptations. But the joy of my love for Jill motivated me to live a certain way. I was patient and persevering, having her in mind with every decision I made. In an even greater way, we live for the day of Christ's coming, patiently waiting. Our love for him motivates us to live not overcome by our circumstances or emotions, but looking unto Jesus at all times, we can have a calm and patient spirit.

Through Diligence

The Christian life is not theoretical. We must do our heart homework. We must not just check boxes. We must all learn to lead and be providers and not merely consumers. Peter returns to his theme of our need to "make every effort" to grow your faith (*cf* 1:5, 10). Peter calls us to be diligent.

2 Peter 3:14b | Be diligent to be found by him.

When I think of diligence versus coasting in the Christian life, I think of thanksgiving dinner. Mom gets up early. She's already prepared for days. But she's the one who a month ago was planning the meal. She puts the turkey in the oven and bastes it. She's prepared the pumpkin pie and the chocolate pie and the pecan pie. So many, many hours have gone into this meal. Mom, as the provider, is glad to sacrifice. Then the consumers arrive. "Ding-dong" goes the front door. A line of hungry relatives arrives. Somehow dad and the kids skedaddle to the wafting aroma of roasted turkey and stuffing. Mouthwatering morsels are inhaled in minutes. And what took mom twenty-five hours to plan, and cook is enveloped within a half hour. Then comes the football game and the nap. Such is the life of a consumer.

Spiritually, we may begin as consumers, and of course we always need to be consumers of the word, but we need to move on from being spoon-fed to feeding ourselves and teaching others. We need to not just be a consumer but a provider. Are you diligent? Do you study the Bible for yourself, or is all you get on Sunday morning for an hour?

To grow in Christ takes diligence. Have you learned to walk and feed yourself spiritually? Don't stay a baby. Are you diligent in the word each day? You will know if you are diligent because if you miss a day, you really feel it. The word keeps your spirit encouraged by the Holy Spirit. When you are not in God's word, you feel the flesh rising up within you. You can't grow without a constant, regular habit of having a quiet time each day.

Are you diligent in fellowship? That means you get here early and stay late. It's rare that you come in late to church, and if you do, you vow never to do it again, just because you don't want to miss the fellowship and the corporate worship.

Are you diligent in prayer? What a joy to pray without ceasing! Are you diligent in discipleship—meeting and encouraging and studying the Bible together.

Through Holiness

What a joy that the Lamb of God who is without spot or blemish gives us his holiness, his righteousness, his heart.

> **2 Peter 3:14c** | Be diligent to be found by him without spot or blemish.

Our diligence is to be aimed at being unblemished and unspotted from the world. False teachers are "blots and blemishes" (*cf* 2:14) so true believers are to be without spot and blemish. We are called to "be found by him" pursuing holiness at Christ's coming. The Bible teaches that the one who is truly justified in Christ is not only perfect before his throne by the righteousness of Christ (Rom 8:1) but also has a new nature that motivates the believer to pursue the righteous way of thinking and living in his heart and life (Eze 36:25-27; Jn 3:3). Consider the truth of the apostle John.

> *1 John 3:9* | No one born of God makes a practice of sinning, for God's seed abides in him, and he cannot keep on sinning because he has been born of God.

Are you advancing and progressing in your holiness? Are you addressing any spots or blemishes in your personal life, your thought life? Make your calling and election sure. If these qualities of holiness are in you and abounding it is certain that you will never fall away as a pretender (*cf* 1:10). So be diligent to live out your standing in Christ (*cf* 1:1).

Through Peace

We are to be diligent, exerting our effort to be at peace with God and with each other.

> **2 Peter 3:14d** | And at peace.

Many Christians have heads filled with Bible knowledge but are tossed about by anxiety and hurt and bitterness and despair. Real Christian maturity is not measured by our doctrinal theories, but our internal rest in Jesus Christ. Are you advancing in the peace of the Holy Spirit? Put off sin and put on the word of God until you come to experience the "peace that passes all understanding" (Phil 4:7) and the "joy unspeakable and full of glory" (1 Pet 1:8).

PROGRESS IN YOUR WISDOM (3:15-17)

Growing in Christ means that we work on our heart and our walk, and this requires that we study the word and experience stability in our lives.

With Steadfastness

Peter tells us now to study God's word with joy, since there are those who will try to twist God's word and say God has forgotten his promises. The false teachers will say the Bible is not literal and historical, but just a compilation of made-up stories to help us feel better. We need to study it knowing it is indeed historical, and that God's promises are true. He is patient in his calling of the lost to himself.

2 Peter 3:15a | And count the patience of our Lord as salvation.

Notice, as you study God's word, you see his nature as patient and kind and compassionate as he waits on sinners to come to him in salvation. Christians should regard God's patience with joy, knowing that he is daily adding to his family until it is complete.[137] God will bring the world to an end soon enough. Until that time, be steadfast in rejoicing in his patience as you study God's word. God's word helps us experience God's compassion and be filled with joy at the patience of God to wait for salvation to have its full effect on a lost and dying world.

With Study

If we are going to grow in our faith we have to "supplement" our faith with the knowledge and wisdom that comes from applying the word of God. When we read the word, we must be careful not just to be satisfied with knowing it intellectually, though we should do that. But just as important is that we walk in the word and let it draw us closer to our God who gave it to us.

Let us be careful not to study the end times prophecies as mere speculation, and instead let the word lead us to revere and worship the Lord for his patience. Instead of speculation we need to have devotion.

---

[137] MacArthur, *2 Peter and Jude*, 134.

Paul's letters were a specific part of Scripture utilized by false teachers to twist the Scriptures and confuse people.

> **2 Peter 3:15b-16** | Just as our beloved brother Paul also wrote to you according to the wisdom given him, **16** as he does in all his letters when he speaks in them of these matters. There are some things in them that are hard to understand, which the ignorant and unstable twist to their own destruction, as they do the other Scriptures.

Appreciation. The fact that Peter placed Paul's writings on a par with the rest of the Scriptures clearly affirms that Paul wrote divinely inspired truth (*cf* 1:20–21; 1 Thess 2:13; 2 Tim 3:16–17). The New Testament writers were aware that they were writing the word of God, as surely as the Old Testament prophets were.[138] Peter and Paul likely worked together in Rome when 2 Peter was written. The first epistle of Clement suggests, they worked together in Rome at the end of their lives (5:2-5).[139] They were both looking for Jesus to come again in their lifetime. Peter said that Paul's writings wrote with the same inspiration as the "other Scriptures" of the Old Testament.

Apostasy. What exactly is Peter alluding to when he says some wolf-like false pastors were "twist the Scriptures"? Peter probably is alluding to Paul's doctrine of justification by faith which was, we know, twisted by unscrupulous teachers to mean that once justified a man could do what he liked with impunity.[140] After all, when we sin, Paul says, "grace abounds" (Rom 5:20). They were willing to twist God's word, missing Paul's own commentary on his words.

> *Romans 6:1-2* | What shall we say then? Are we to continue in sin that grace may abound? ² By no means! How can we who died to sin still live in it?

Self-aggrandizing preachers in Peter's day were twisting the word of God to their own destruction. Then and now they teach God's people to sin whether by giving subtle and sanctified excuses for sin ("We all sin anyway, don't we?), or teaching outright antinomianism ("Since grace abounds, let's sin all the more"). The false teachers confused true

---

[138] MacArthur, *2 Peter and Jude*, 136.
[139] Green, *2 Peter and Jude*, 170.
[140] Ibid., 171.

believers and made them unstable in their faith. Instead of looking with holiness, they were distracted by loose living.

Application. We need to be wise! Don't be distracted by false teachers. If a church starts approving of lawlessness, you should leave. Today churches are affirming the lawless practices of homosexuality and gender blending. There is confusing in the pulpits. Let us not be confused. Gender blending does not make a boy into a girl or a girl into a boy. It just makes the parents who support that confusion into those who commit child abuse.

The way to wisdom is the study of God's word. Readers have sometimes been mistaken that Peter himself somehow found parts of Paul's letters hard to understand, but in fact this is false. He clearly suggests that such passages are open to misinterpretation only by the ignorant— "uninstructed and unstable" people. In other words, the false teachers, for all their pretensions to be teachers, had never taken the trouble to acquire a broad, sound knowledge of apostolic teaching.[141] The only defense against these kinds of wolves is a rich and broad study of God's word.

With Stability

As in the first chapter, Peter warns the believer not to "lose your own stability." When we see Christians who fall away and are lawless, we might fall with them if we are focused on mere the actions of sinful men instead of the mighty God.

> **2 Peter 3:17** | You therefore, beloved, knowing this beforehand, take care that you are not carried away with the error of lawless people and lose your own stability.

With Peter's call to "stability," Peter comes full circle—not only in this letter, but in his life.[142] He's told us that it is the Scripture that brings us stability—a more sure word of prophecy than miracles like the transfiguration (1:19).

We must have our focus set on the Lord who never fails. That's where stability comes from. As with the recipients of Peter's letter, we all go through difficult times. Those trials seem to hit us even harder when the source of the struggles comes from somewhere or someone

---

[141] Bauckham, *2 Peter–Jude*, 106–107.
[142] Helm, *1 & 2 Peter and Jude*, 273.

close to us. We hear about the "lawless" activity of so-called Christians that we've trusted, and it can bring great instability, as Peter says. People we trusted and followed now have a rift in their marriage. An unwed daughter is unexpectedly pregnancy. You find out about an abusive relationship in the life of someone you have cared about. Other times it's in the area of doctrine. Someone you love starts believing lies. Wolves enter into churches and start deceiving your loved ones. Their lawless activity can really discourage us and bring instability.

To guard against that kind of instability that can carry us away—both in our families and our churches—God's people need to know who the Lord is on a very personal and intimate level. Our knowledge of God through his word is the first line of defense against the conflicts and instability that threatens to tear us apart.

PROGRESS IN YOUR WITNESS (3:18)

As Peter writes his last words before he and his wife are crucified, he urges us, as he did in the beginning of his letter, to grow! We witness our progress in Christ by God's grace and for his glory.

The Witness of God's Grace

We are to grow! Grow means "to advance or increase in the sphere of something."[143] We are to progress and advance in knowing Christ.

> **2 Peter 3:18a** | But grow in the grace and knowledge of our Lord and Savior Jesus Christ.

Knowledge here is not merely information, but a spiritual intimacy with Jesus. A spiritual understanding of Christ is the only bulwark against spiritual deception. The only way not to become unstable (3:17), is the way of growth in grace and knowledge. It is through personal encounter with Jesus as Savior and Lord that the Christian life begins. It is through constant contact with him in both those capacities that Christian character develops.[144]

Peter grew from a headstrong Galilean to a humble apostle—from a simple fisherman to a legendary fisher of men. We, too, can follow him on his remarkable journey of spiritual growth as we heed his warnings, recall his reminders, and embrace the divine promises he

---

[143] MacArthur, *2 Peter and Jude*, 137.
[144] Green, *2 Peter and Jude*, 175.

describes, applying diligence and hope and relying on the provision of the Holy Spirit. When we do this, we will be able to defeat false doctrine, avoid moral compromise, and join Peter in his passionate praise of our Lord and Savior Jesus Christ: "all glory to God!"[145]

The Witness of God's Glory

Peter can almost taste the glory of heaven as he is ready to depart, that he suddenly bursts into singing.

2 Peter 3:18b | To him be the glory both now and to the day of eternity. Amen.

This song of praise contains the final words we hear from Peter on this earth. In writing them, it is as if he has already arrived. Imagine the joy of singing your way into heaven.[146]

To give glory is to reflect the character of God and to give praise to God. It's to "give the right opinion of" someone. We are called to give God all the glory for what he's doing now, and what he will do with us in the eternal state.

Conclusion

"Glory," shouts Peter. "To him be glory both now and to the day of eternity. Amen." So Peter takes his readers back to the Mount of Transfiguration, where Jesus' glory had been displayed. He saw the glory of Christ unveiled. "To him be glory!" he exclaims. Then he adds his last "Amen." With that, Peter puts down his pen. We have heard the last of him—for now!

One day, the expected knock came at his door. Nero's attention had been drawn to him at last. He was arrested and sentenced to death by crucifixion. It was a cruel way to die. It is said he didn't feel worthy to be crucified in the manner of his Lord, so he was granted an upside down crucifixion.

The end came soon enough. The gates of glory opened, and Peter was absent from the body and present with the Lord. We can almost hear him, his voice rising in unison with all of the other ransomed saints of God: "To him be glory both now and forever, and ever, and ever!" Amen and amen![147]

---

[145] Swindoll, *Insights on James and 1 & 2 Peter*, 330.
[146] Helm, *1 & 2 Peter and Jude*, 275.
[147] Phillips, *Exploring the Epistles of Peter*, 2 Pe 3:17–18.

SELECTED BIBLIOGRAPHY

In order of appearance in the commentary

COMMENTARIES

D. Edmond Hiebert, *Second Peter and Jude: An Expositional Commentary* (Greenville, SC: Bob Jones University Press, 1989).

Allen Black and Mark C. Black, *1 & 2 Peter*, The College Press NIV Commentary (Joplin, MO: College Press Pub., 1998).

David H. Wheaton, "2 Peter," in *New Bible Commentary: 21st Century Edition*, ed. D. A. Carson et al., 4th ed. (Leicester, England; Downers Grove, IL: Inter-Varsity Press, 1994).

John F. MacArthur Jr., *2 Peter and Jude*, MacArthur New Testament Commentary (Chicago: Moody Publishers, 2005).

Charles R. Swindoll, *Insights on James and 1 & 2 Peter*, Swindoll's New Testament Commentary (Grand Rapids, MI: Zondervan, 2010).

Thomas R. Schreiner, *1, 2 Peter, Jude*, vol. 37, The New American Commentary (Nashville: Broadman & Holman Publishers, 2003).

Stephen W. Paine, "The Second Epistle to Peter," in *The Wycliffe Bible Commentary*, eds. Charles F. Pfeiffer and Everett F. Harrison (Chicago: Moody, 1962).

Michael Green, *2 Peter and Jude: An Introduction and Commentary*, vol. 18, Tyndale New Testament Commentaries (Downers Grove, IL: InterVarsity Press, 1987).

J. Daryl Charles and Erland Waltner, *1–2 Peter, Jude* (Scottdale, PA: Herald Press, 1999).

Richard J. Bauckham, *Jude, 2 Peter* (Waco, TX: Word Books, 1983).
David R. Helm, *1 & 2 Peter and Jude: Sharing Christ's Sufferings*, Preaching the Word (Wheaton, IL: Crossway Books, 2008).
David Walls and Max Anders, *I & II Peter, I, II & III John, Jude*, vol. 11, Holman New Testament Commentary (Nashville, TN: Broadman & Holman Publishers, 1999).
William Barclay, *The Letters of James and Peter*, 2nd ed., The Daily Study Bible Series (Philadelphia: Westminster, 1960).
Andrew M. Mbuvi, *Jude and 2 Peter, A New Covenant Commentary*, (Eugene, OR: Cascade Books, 2015).
Douglas Harink, 1 & 2 Peter (Grand Rapids, MI: Brazos Press, 2009).
Bruce B. Barton, *1 & 2 Peter and Jude—Life Application Bible Commentary* (Carol Stream, IL: Tyndale, 1995).
John Phillips, *Exploring the Epistles of Peter: An Expository Commentary*, The John Phillips Commentary Series (Kregel Publications; WORDsearch Corp., 2009).
H.A. Ironside, *Illustrations of Bible Truth* (Chicago: Moody Press, 1945).
Archibald Geikie Brown, *The Devil's Mission of Amusement: A Protest* (London: Morgan & Scott, 1889). See chapter on "Amusing the Goats or Feeding the Sheep."
Richard J. Bauckham, *2 Peter–Jude*, ed. David A. Hubbard and Ralph P. Martin, Word Biblical Themes (Grand Rapids, MI: Zondervan Academic, 1990).
R. C. H. Lenski, *The Interpretation of the Epistles of St. Peter, St. John and St. Jude* (Minneapolis: Augsburg, 1961).
Dieudonné Tamfu, *2 Peter and Jude* (Carlisle, UK: HippoBooks, 2018).

SERMONS

Charles Spurgeon, "The Wailing of Risca" in *Metropolitan Tabernacle Pulpit*, Vol 7 (London: Passmore and Alabaster, 1861), 9.
Timothy J. Keller, "The Dangerous Life" Studies in 2 Peter—August 15, 1993 from 2 Peter 2:1–9, *The Timothy Keller Sermon Archive* (New York City: Redeemer Presbyterian Church, 2013).
Adrian Rogers, "Three Marks of an Apostate," in *Adrian Rogers Sermon Archive* (Signal Hill, CA: Rogers Family Trust, 2017).

ANCIENT SOURCES

Origen, *Fathers of the Church: A New Translation,* "Sermons on Leviticus 4.4.2" (Washington, D.C.: Catholic University of America Press, 1947–).

Flavius Josephus. *Antiquities of the Jews* (A.D. 93).

Saint Augustine Bishop of Hippo, *The Confessions of St. Augustine,* trans. E. B. Pusey (Oak Harbor, WA: Logos Research Systems, Inc., 1996).

Irenaeus of Lyons, *Against Heresies* 1.1.2, in *The Ante-Nicene Fathers: Translations of the Writings of the Fathers down to AD 325,* ed. Alexander Roberts et al.; vol. 1, *The Apostolic Fathers, Justin Martyr, Irenaeus,* American reprint ed. (New York: Charles Scribner's Sons, 1899).

Eusebius, *The Ecclesiastical History* (313 A.D.).

Jerome, *De Viris Illustribus (On Illustrious Men).*

Richard Baxter, *The Saints Everlasting Rest* (Leeds, England: Davies and Booth Publishing, 1814).

BIOGRAPHICAL

R.A. Torrey, *Why God Used D. L. Moody* (Edinburgh, UK: CrossReach Publications, 2015).

DICTIONARIES

J. D. G. Dunn, "Repentance," in *New Bible Dictionary,* ed. D. R. W. Wood et al. (Leicester, England; Downers Grove, IL: InterVarsity Press, 1996).

W. E. Vine, *An Expository Dictionary of New Testament Words,* 4 vols. (London: Oliphants, 1940; reprint, Chicago: Moody, 1985).

NEW TESTAMENT

J M. R. Vincent, *Word Studies in the New Testament* (McLean, VA: MacDonald Publishing Company, 1886).

J. A. Bengel, *Gnomon Novi Testament.*

F.F. Bruce. *The New Testament Documents: Are They Reliable?* (Grand Rapids, MI: Eerdmans Publishing Company, 2003).

BACKGROUNDS

James M. Starr, *Sharers in Divine Nature: 2 Peter 1:4 in Its Hellenistic Context (Coniectanea Biblica New Testament Series, 33)* (Stockholm: Almqvist & Wiksell International, 2000).

Marva J. Dawn, *Powers, Weakness, and the Tabernacling of God* (Grand Rapids, MI: Wm. B. Eerdmans Publishing, 2001).

John Howard Yoder, *The Politics of Jesus: Vicit Agnus Noster*, 2nd ed. (Grand Rapids: Eerdmans, 1994), 134–61; and Marva J. Dawn, *Powers, Weakness, and the Tabernacling of God* (Grand Rapids: Eerdmans, 2001).

Bernd Wannenwetsch, "Representing the Absent in the City: Prolegomena to a Negative Political Theology according to Revelation 21," in *God, Truth, and Witness: Engaging Stanley Hauerwas*, ed. L. Gregory Jones, Reinhard Hütter, and C. Rosalee Velloso Ewell (Grand Rapids: Brazos, 2005).

Christian Smith and Melinda Lundquist Denton, *Soul Searching: The Religious and Spiritual Lives of American Teenagers* (Oxford, UK: Oxford University Press, 2009).

William Dembski in July Roys, *The Evolution Litmus Test.* (Chicago: The Roys Report, December 5, 2014), julieroys.com/the-evolution-litmus-test.

Stephen C. Meyer, *Aliens, the Multiverse, or God?* (Seattle, WA: Discovery Institute, December 22, 2021), discovery.org/v/aliens-multiverse-god.

Kenneth Chang, *Gauging Age of Universe Becomes More Precise* (New York: New York Times Newspaper, March 9, 2008).

John C. Whitcomb, Jr., and Henry M. Morris, *The Genesis Flood* (Grand Rapids: Baker, 1961).

THEOLOGY

Bruce L. Kelly, *Christian Theology in Plain Language* (Nashville, TN: Word Books, 1985).

J. Daryl Charles, *Virtue Amidst Vice: The Catalog of Virtues in 2 Peter 1* (London: Sheffield Academic Press, 1997).

TOPICAL

Timothy S. Lane, *Unstuck: A Nine-Step Journey to Change that Lasts* (Epsom, UK: The Good Book Company, 2019).

Abraham Lincoln in Richard Stearns, *Unfinished: Filling the Hole in Our Gospel* (Nashville, TN: Thomas Nelson, 2014).

Mark Jobe. *Unstuck: Out of Your Cave, Into Your Call* (Chicago: Moody Publishers, 2014).

Warren Dunham Foster. *Heroines of Modern Religion* (New York: Sturgis & Walton Co., 1913).

Jerry Bridges, *Trusting God: Even When Life Hurts* (Colorado Springs, CO: Nav Press, 1988).

WENATCHEE, WASHINGTON

You may obtain this, and many other fine resources made available by Proclaim Publishers by contacting us:

Web:
proclaimpublishers.com

Email:
contact@proclaimpublishers.com

Postal Mail:
Proclaim Publishers
PO Box 2082
Wenatchee, WA 98807

Soli Deo Gloria

www.ingramcontent.com/pod-product-compliance
Lightning Source LLC
Chambersburg PA
CBHW022116040426
42450CB00006B/722